THE ESSENTIAL
AIR FRYER
COOKBOOK
FOR BEGINNERS

THE ESSENTIAL AIR FRYER COOKBOOK FOR BEGINNERS

EASY, FOOLPROOF RECIPES FOR YOUR AIR FRYER

LAURIE FLEMING

PHOTOGRAPHY BY DARREN MUIR

ROCKRIDGE
PRESS

For general information on our other products and services or to obtain technical support, please contact our Customer Care Department within the United States at (866) 744-2665, or outside the United States at (510) 253-0500.

Rockridge Press publishes its books in a variety of electronic and print formats. Some content that appears in print may not be available in electronic books, and vice versa.

Interior and Cover Designer: John Clifford
Art Producer: Hannah Dickerson
Editor: Marjorie DeWitt

Photography © 2019 Darren Muir.
Author photo courtesy of Betsy Brody.

Cover: Sweet Potato French Fries

ISBN: Print 978-1-64611-151-0 | eBook 978-1-64611-153-4

R0

To my two amazing sons, Ethan and Jason, who always pushed me to try another recipe, make another amazing dessert or just make an extra piece of chicken.

Contents

< Buffalo Chicken Wings,
  page 64

Introduction

Welcome to the wonderful world of air fryer cooking! As the proud new owner of an air fryer, you are probably wondering where to start. You may be looking for tips on how to use your new appliance or for new recipes. I was once in the same position you are now. By sharing my own journey with the air fryer, I hope to help guide and inform your new adventure with air fryer cooking.

Back in 2016, I received my first air fryer as a gift. At the time, I was homeschooling my children, and they were participating in oodles of after-school activities. Our days were packed, and I was faced with the challenge of getting dinner on the table. While grabbing fast food would have been an easy choice, I chose to cook with the air fryer, because we were trying to teach our children the importance of family meals and making healthy choices.

I had a rough start using the air fryer. Air fryers weren't that popular yet, so there wasn't much guidance out there. The recipes I was able to find didn't always work out. As a result, I made a few horrible meals—or, as my kids would say, inedible. I had months of trial and error. I would often make a recipe in the oven and in the air fryer, and I would—more often than not—throw away the air fried food. The chefs on the infomercials made it seem so easy.

I took this as a challenge. Soon, I was mastering the art of the air fryer and enjoying it. I began sharing my tried-and-true recipes with my friends in an online Facebook group, and I loved trying and sharing theirs, too.

My first recipe, which I worked days and days on, was very simple: cinnamon rolls. I was convinced that if you could cook in the air fryer, you should also be able to bake in the air fryer. I had never been much of a baker, but I have now baked hundreds of cakes, muffins, brownies, and cookies using my air fryer.

As my air fryer baking story attests, air fryers today have many functions. They are not just for frying. You can bake, grill, steam, roast, and toast all in your air fryer. Because they have so many useful functions, air fryers have become wildly popular, and there is a wide range of air fryers on the market. For the recipes in this book, I used a 5.8-quart basket air fryer. I find that this is a common size and style for beginners, but all the recipes can be easily adapted to different models. That said, I am currently the proud owner of six air fryers, all different models. I blog about my cooking adventures—with all my air fryers!—at ForkToSpoon.com.

With this book, I wanted to transfer my hard-earned knowledge to you in a clear and useful guide to your new appliance, so you can avoid some of the struggles I experienced early on. I have included all the information needed to get started using an air fryer: how it works and how to use it, as well as how to care for and clean it. Best of all, I have selected 75 of my favorite easy air fryer recipes, all of which use inexpensive, easy-to-find ingredients.

I hope that with this information, you will enjoy your air fryer as much as I enjoy mine.

AIR FRYER 101

This chapter will give you a basic understanding of how your air fryer works and what your air fryer can do for you. One of the biggest myths about the air fryer is that it is used only for frying foods. The truth is that it does so much more. In this chapter, you'll learn how to use your air fryer's functions, whether grilling, baking, roasting, frying, or steaming. You will also find safety and cleaning information, as well as indispensable tips for air fryer success. Let's get started.

WHY AIR FRY?

Air fryers are all the rage now, but they have been around for some time. In 2005, the original patent for a commercial air fryer was filed; this patent was for a large air fryer, which was marketed to the food industry. In 2010, air fryers began to be sold for household use, and today there are many brands of air fryers to choose from.

The reason why air fryers are so popular is that they allow you to substitute high-fat deep-frying with healthy air frying. The air fryer cooks by circulating hot air around the food. This allows you to make crispy food with little or no oil, which is much healthier than deep-frying and even sautéing. The constant circulation of high heat in an air fryer triggers a chemical reaction called the Maillard reaction, which occurs between a food's sugars and amino acids and results in it being browned, crispy, and flavorful.

Some of the many benefits to air frying follow.

HEALTH

Air frying requires very little oil, usually just a spritz or two. Because air frying uses dramatically less oil, air fried foods have fewer calories and less fat than traditionally deep-fried or sautéed foods.

CONVENIENCE

Air fryer cooking is quick and easy. I began using an air fryer because my family's hectic schedule made preparing meals with long cooking times difficult. Once I got the hang of it, air frying changed my life. I can now get home-cooked meals on the table in minutes. The convenience of air fryers does not only benefit busy families like mine; it also benefits single people, older adults, couples, college students—everyone, really!

QUICKER MEALS

Cooking in the air fryer takes less time than in a traditional oven since the unit is smaller and the air fryer is equipped with a mechanical fan that continually circulates very hot air throughout the cooking chamber. The cooking time for most meals is reduced by an average of 30 percent, and that's not counting the time you save from not needing to preheat an oven. You will soon find that you can grill a steak in under 6 minutes, bake chicken tenders in 8 minutes, and have dinner on the table more quickly than ordering takeout.

EASY TO USE

Once you begin cooking with an air fryer, you will be amazed at how easy it is to use. Where you once had to use a whole bunch of different appliances and stock your kitchen with cabinets full of pans for frying, grilling, steaming, roasting, and baking, with an air fryer you can cook most foods right in the basket and achieve the same delicious results. This book makes air fryer cooking even easier with simple, step-by-step recipes, as well as tips and tricks that will have you on the path to being an air fryer pro in no time.

ENERGY EFFICIENT

Because your air fryer is versatile and compact, and decreases cooking times, you will most likely reduce the amount of energy you use to cook. You often don't need to preheat your air fryer at all, and if you do preheat, it takes only 2 to 5 minutes, as opposed to 15 to 20 minutes for a traditional oven. Furthermore, you will not have to heat the entire oven for one or two pieces of baked chicken or a small batch of muffins.

EASY CLEANUP

Air fryers require hardly any cleanup. There are only two parts of an air fryer that need to be consistently cleaned: the basket and the drawer. Both are easy to clean with dish soap and a sponge or by running them through the dishwasher. There is no need to spend hours soaking and scouring baking sheets, frying pans, and grill surfaces. The outside surface of the air fryer and the heating element only need to be wiped down periodically. Furthermore, because air fryer baking pans are smaller than conventional baking pans, they easily fit in the dishwasher.

THE AIR FRYER

Getting to know the basic features of your air fryer will help ensure your success. While each brand and model is a little bit different—some have pre-programmed cooking options, some have manual temperature and timer dials, and some have a digital control panel—they do share many common traits. The diagram and explanations below will give you an overview of your air fryer's basic features (consult your manual for more detailed information about your particular model).

AIR FRYER BASKET

This is the part of the air fryer that you will fill with the food you're cooking. The important things to remember about the air fryer basket are (1) be sure to spray it with olive oil before you load it up, which will help prevent the food from sticking, and (2) don't overload the basket or your food will not brown and cook evenly—this is especially true with anything that is cooked in pieces (French fries, chicken wings, asparagus, steak tips, etc.).

AIR FRYER DRAWER

The air fryer basket sits inside the air fryer drawer. These two pieces snap together during cooking but can be separated by pressing a button at the top of the drawer handle after you remove the air fryer drawer from the air fryer. You will want to release the basket from the drawer before you turn out (or remove) the basket's contents. You'll also want to separate the basket and the drawer for cleaning.

HEATING ELEMENT AND FAN

The heating element sits directly above the air fryer basket and looks like a burner coil on an electric stove. Above the heating element is a mechanical fan, which pushes the hot air around the air fryer.

The combination of the top-down heat, the circulating hot air, and the small cooking space speeds up cooking.

AIR INLET

This is where the air comes into the air fryer, which allows your air fryer to stay cool during the cooking time. If the air inlet is blocked, the air fryer will overheat. Be sure to keep this area clear.

AIR OUTLET OPENINGS

This is where the air leaves the air fryer as it is cooking. Sometimes you will see steam come out of this vent. Remember that the air and steam released through this outlet can be hot. For this reason, do not put your air fryer underneath your cabinets or too near the wall because the heat can cause damage to paint and other surfaces. Never store anything directly on top of your air fryer.

TEMPERATURE CONTROL

Depending on your brand and model, this may be a manual dial or a digital setting on a control panel. This is where you set the temperature for your food. Most air fryers have a heating range of 200°F to 400°F.

TIMER

This is where you set the cook time for your food. It could be a manual dial or part of a digital control panel.

POWER LIGHT

The power light comes on when your air fryer is on.

HEATING UP LIGHT

The heating up light indicates that the air fryer is heating up. (Only some models have this feature.)

FUNCTIONS OF YOUR AIR FRYER

Your trusty air fryer can fry, grill, bake, roast, steam, and toast. It will not only save you time but also a ton of counter and cabinet space. So much so that you might soon be giving away your oven-size pans!

Some models of air fryers have presets for specific functions or foods. If your model does not have presets, then the temperature, type of food, and food's preparation determine the function. For example, I roast chicken breasts at 370°F, I grill a whole steak at 400°F, and I bake cookies at 320°F.

FRY

Frying traditionally means cooking with very hot oil. Two of the most common examples are deep-frying—when you cook food by submerging it in a large quantity of hot oil—and sautéing—when you use one or more tablespoons of hot oil or melted butter in the bottom of a frying pan to cook your food. The high temperature of the oil or butter causes the outside of the food to get brown and crispy and the inside of the food to remain tender and moist. This is generally thought of as one of the unhealthiest ways to cook, since fried food absorbs a lot of fat in the cooking process. So, even if you start out with a healthy food, like a chicken breast, by the end of the frying process your chicken will be high in calories and fat.

Like traditional frying, air frying uses high heat, but instead of using hot oil to cook the food, it uses hot air, which is continuously circulated in a small chamber. This achieves the same effect as cooking with oil without the fatty calories or the mess. Most fried foods made in the air fryer are simply sprayed with a small amount of olive oil (or another oil with a high smoke point), if oil is used at all.

A few of the many foods that you can fry more healthily in an air fryer include fried eggs, Sweet Potato French Fries (page 102), onion rings, and Buffalo Chicken Wings (page 64). Using the fry function on your air fryer is also a great way to heat up frozen foods.

GRILL

Grilling is when the heat from a charcoal or gas flame is applied from below and sears the outside of the food quickly, trapping most of the juices inside. Grilling is generally considered to be a healthy option for preparing meats because it doesn't require a lot of oil or fat.

When you grill in your air fryer, you also use high heat—usually temperatures between 370°F and 400°F. And, like barbecue grilling, you need only a few tablespoons of olive oil to produce a slice of juicy meat. All of the meat I've cooked in the air fryer has been equal to, if not better than, grilled meats. Air fryer hamburgers and hot dogs are amazingly delicious—so juicy and flavorful!

BAKE

The most surprising feature of the air fryer is the baking function. Baking uses indirect dry heat to cook food. The heat starts cooking the food on the edges and the surface, cooking it from the outside to the center to produce a thoroughly cooked item. You can bake anything in the air fryer that you would bake in a traditional oven; however, in air fryer baking, the temperature is usually about 30 percent lower.

Baking times for air fryers can vary slightly from model to model. So, for your first few air fryer baking projects, I recommend that you closely watch the cooking time and keep brief notes, which will help you learn exact baking times for your particular machine. Also, keep some aluminum foil handy to cover the top of your baked goods in case the top is browning before the middle is cooked.

ROAST

Roasting is a lot like baking. Both methods cook food using indirect dry heat. Roasting is the preferred term when this method is used to cook meat and vegetables, while baking is the preferred term for foods made from a batter or dough (although sometimes chicken and fish dishes are baked as a healthier alternative to frying). Temperatures for roasting are usually a little higher than baking, but they can vary depending on what is being cooked.

STEAM

Steaming means that the food is cooked by the heat from the steam produced by boiling water. In conventional cooking, this is usually done by setting a steaming rack or a double boiler over boiling water. Air fryers do a great job steaming all kinds of vegetables, including broccoli and spinach.

TOAST

Another surprising function of the air fryer is that it toasts bread, English muffins, or bagels. Anything you use your toaster for now, the air fryer can also do. Toasting is different from baking, as the toast becomes browned from radiant heat. This is a perfect job for the air fryer because the heating source is generally located directly above the basket where the food is positioned.

GET TO AIR FRYING!

When you are preparing to use your air fryer for the first time, you might be scared about messing up or forgetting something. Use the step-by-step guide below as a checklist when you get started. Refer to it as often as you need when you are tackling your first few recipes, and before you know it, you'll be on your way to becoming an air fryer pro.

1. **Unbox your air fryer.**

   Pay careful attention that all the parts are accounted for. Air fryer parts are sometimes very small, so make sure you don't lose any in the unpacking process.

2. **Read the manual.**

   The first thing I suggest is that you read your manual, which may sound like a daunting task, but all air fryers are a little different, even though they operate in mostly the same way. It's important to become familiar with the parts and instructions for your particular model.

3. **Wash the air fryer basket and the air fryer drawer.**

   Since these are the parts that will come in contact with food, wash them using soap, water, and a nonabrasive sponge. This will help get rid of any residue from the manufacturing process.

4. **Season the air fryer basket.**

   Your basket is a lot like a cast iron pan, and if you season it before the first use, it will last longer. It will also help prevent food from sticking to your basket.

   Since your basket is in direct contact with heat for extended periods of time, I suggest you rub the basket down with coconut oil and then turn the heat to the highest temperature on your model (probably 400°F). Let the basket heat up with the coconut oil for about 5 minutes, then let the basket cool down to room temperature. Now it's ready to use.

5. **Preheat, if necessary.**

   This will depend on your model. Preheating means heating the cooking chamber to the temperature that the recipe calls for before cooking. So, if you are preparing a steak and the recipe recommends a cooking temperature of 400°F, you would preheat your air fryer at 400°F for 2 to 5 minutes (or according to the manufacturer's instructions). Generally, I do not find it necessary to preheat. In the recipes in this book, I will only recommend preheating for a few specific dishes, but I suggest that you read the manual for your particular model and follow the manufacturer's instructions for best results.

6. Prepare your ingredients.

It's important in air frying that whatever you're cooking is cut to the same size, so that all the pieces cook evenly.

7. Spray the air fryer basket with oil.

If you're cooking food directly in the air fryer basket, you need to spray your basket with oil. Yes, your basket (if you followed my advice) will already be seasoned, but the next best thing to keeping the basket in great shape is spraying it down with oil to ensure that the food doesn't stick. (Do not use nonstick cooking spray to spray your basket because it can degrade the surface of the basket.)

8. Place your food in the air fryer basket.

Make sure not to overcrowd the basket. Aim for placing the food in a single layer. This will help your food cook and crisp evenly. Too much food in the basket can cause the food in the middle or the bottom of the basket to be soft, while the food on the top and sides is more crisp.

9. Spray food with oil, if needed.

Especially for foods with a breaded coating like pork or chicken cutlets, you will need to spray your food with a coating of oil. The oil coating will ensure that your breading is crisp and flavorful. Powdery, white, undercooked breading is one of the most common problems beginners encounter with air frying—and it doesn't taste very good. So for these items, don't forget to spray them generously with oil.

10. Set the temperature.

See the charts on pages 18 to 25 for suggested cooking times or follow the recipe's temperature setting. (If you've already preheated your air fryer, skip this step.)

11. Set the timer for half of the cooking time, then flip or shake.

I begin by setting my timer for half of the total cooking time, because I always flip (if meat) or shake (foods that are in small pieces, like French fries or other cut vegetables) halfway during the cooking process to ensure even cooking. If you are cooking something breaded, it is important to generously spray the top with oil after you flip it so that it browns evenly. Flipping or shaking halfway through cooking is critical for best results. Be sure to reset the timer for the remaining cooking time after you have flipped or shaken your ingredients.

12. Remove your cooked food from the air fryer basket.

When the food is completely cooked, use tongs or a spatula to remove the food—or silicone oven mitts if you are removing a hot pan—because the air fryer basket will be hot and touching it will result in burns.

The air fryer drawer captures any drippings from the food cooked in the air fryer basket. Do not turn the food out of the basket when the drawer and basket are locked together, as you risk making a big mess. First, release the basket from the drawer by pushing the button at the top of the drawer handle, then you can turn out the food from the basket onto a plate or into a bowl. You can either pour the liquid captured in the drawer over the plated food as a sauce, if desired, or safely discard the contents of the drawer.

AIR FRYER SAFETY

Remember to read the manual for important safety precautions before operating your air fryer. Since every model is different, it's important to be familiar with your own air fryer's safety features.

One of the most important aspects of using your air fryer is the location of it. I strongly recommend placing your air fryer on a heat-resistant mat and not directly on the countertop, because the bottom of the air fryer can sometimes get hot. But read your manual first to see what the manufacturer recommends, because some models cannot have anything underneath, as it may interrupt the air flow and cause the air fryer to overheat.

DO NOT ATTEMPT TO CLEAN THE AIR FRYER WHEN IT IS PLUGGED IN OR STILL HOT!

Make sure there is plenty of space around and above your air fryer. It is not a good idea to operate your air fryer directly under a cabinet.

Do not place your air fryer on your stove or on anything that can accidently be turned on, which could cause the air fryer to catch fire. Remember that your air fryer has an electrical cord attached and, therefore, should not be exposed to heat or water.

Remember to unplug your air fryer after each and every use.

CLEANING AND CARING FOR YOUR AIR FRYER

Depending on the model you own, the only thing you'll need to clean after each use is the air fryer basket and the air fryer drawer. The most important thing about cleaning these pieces is to remove the basket from the drawer by pushing the release button (usually at the top of the drawer handle). If you clean these parts after each use, you will have a very clean and long-lasting air fryer.

To clean the interior of the air fryer drawer, use a soft brush and some dish soap. Wipe the outside of the drawer with a nonabrasive sponge (anything abrasive will take off the coating). To clean the air fryer basket, follow the same instructions, using a generous amount of dish soap and a nonabrasive sponge. Rinse the basket and the drawer thoroughly. Hand washing—even though most air fryer baskets and air fryer drawers are dishwasher safe—will provide a longer life for your air fryer.

Occasionally, you will need to wipe down the outside of your air fryer with a damp cloth and a drop of dishwashing liquid. You will also need to wipe off the heating element periodically. Many people don't do this, but you should do it to prevent any greasy build-up inside the machine. To do this, first make sure that your air fryer is completely cooled, turned off, and unplugged, then remove the drawer and the basket and gently wipe the top of the chamber with a damp cloth.

OILS

Even though you need very little—if any—oil to cook in the air fryer, there are some important things about oils to keep in mind.

There is a wide variety of oils to choose from when cooking with an air fryer, but each different kind of oil has different properties, the most important of which is the smoke point, or the point at which oil begins to break down and produce smoke. The air fryer generates high heat; therefore, to prevent smoking up your kitchen, you will want to use an oil that has a high smoke point.

My go-to oil for air frying is olive oil. There are a few different kinds to choose from. "Light" olive oil is a refined olive oil that has a high smoke point and a very mild or neutral flavor. Virgin olive oil also has a high smoke point but more olive oil flavor, and extra-virgin olive oil (EVOO) has the most flavor but a slightly lower smoke point.

In addition to olive oil, the following oils all have a high smoke point and will work well in your air fryer:

Avocado oil

Canola oil

Ghee (clarified butter)

Grapeseed oil

Peanut oil

Sesame oil

I recommend avoiding nonstick cooking spray because it can damage nonstick surfaces, and over time, it can cause peeling of your air fryer basket.

SPRAY IT ON!

One of the great health benefits of air frying is that it uses far less oil than traditional frying. Some air fryer recipes need no oil at all, and some require only a light spray coating to encourage crisping and browning. For this reason, I've found that a good, reusable spray bottle for oil is a must. I recommend that you invest in a food-grade spray bottle made of glass. They are available online and in the kitchenware section of most department stores.

The amount of oil you will need to use depends on what you are cooking, but it will be consistently far less than traditional recipes use. For breaded items, you'll need to spray them with oil so the breading will brown and crisp. This way, you also don't get powdery white patches of uncooked breading, which is not pleasant to eat. For vegetables, you need only a light spritz of oil, if any.

10 TIPS FOR PERFECT AIR FRYING

The following 10 tips will help any new air fryer user. I find that they are the most common problems and questions that arise as you first use your air fryer.

1. **Don't use aerosol spray.**

   One of the most common questions I come across is whether to use aerosol spray in your air fryer. The answer is no. Do not use any aerosol sprays in your air fryer, because they are usually lower quality oil and have additives such as propellants, which can damage your basket. As a result, the coating could come off. And, unfortunately, the coating could come off on your food, making it unsafe to eat. Therefore, before placing your food into the air fryer, simply give it a quick spray of olive oil.

2. **Shake the basket frequently.**

   If you are making diced potatoes, diced chicken, or anything cut up into pieces, remember to shake the basket frequently. This shaking will guarantee the food is evenly cooked, evenly colored, and crispy. All you need to do is pull out the air fryer drawer, give it a few shakes, and put it back in.

3. **Check the temperature and time.**

   Use the recommendations in the recipes and the charts on pages 18 to 25 as you start using your air fryer. But keep in mind that every model is different, so as you make new things, note the time it takes your machine to fully cook the food. Use a food thermometer to check for doneness. It is very dangerous to eat uncooked meat, especially pork and chicken.

4. **Flip baked goods if the middle does not fully cook.**

   When you're baking quick breads, muffins, cakes, and other baked goods, if a toothpick test reveals that the middle isn't done yet at the end of the cook time, just take the bread, cake, etc., out of the pan and flip it. Carefully place it in the basket upside-down and allow it to finish cooking.

5. **Spray generously with oil to avoid white spots on breaded foods.**

   White spots mean that you have not oiled your food enough; this happens on breaded food items.

6. **Use your air fryer to heat frozen foods.**

   The air fryer is a great way to heat up your frozen foods; the general rule is a 30 percent reduction in time.

7. **Don't overcrowd the air fryer basket.**

   If you start to get unevenly cooked food, the problem probably lies with the quantity of food you are making. You need to leave space between food items and not stack the food. Crowding and stacking result in food that cooks unevenly or lacks crispness.

8. **Avoid smoke when cooking bacon.**

   If you get smoke when you are cooking bacon, put a slice of bread on the bottom of the drawer, which will absorb the grease and eliminate the smoking from the air fryer.

9. **Use aluminum foil.**

   Foil is allowed in the air fryer. You can wrap vegetables in foil to steam them, or use it over baked goods, like cakes and pies, to slow browning on the top while the middle cooks.

10. **Use parchment paper.**

    Using parchment paper really helps with cleanup, because you throw it away after use. Perforated parchment paper cut to fit many sizes of air fryer baskets is available. I have not been able to find it in box stores, but it is available on Amazon.

EQUIPMENT

When using an air fryer, there are a few inexpensive pieces of equipment that will help make your experience with the air fryer go more smoothly. I have divided these into two lists: "Need to Have" and "Nice to Have."

NEED TO HAVE

- **OIL SPRAYER:** As you begin air frying, this will become one of the most useful items in your kitchen. Opt for a quality food-grade glass sprayer.

- **SMALL MUFFIN TIN:** Some air fryers come with muffin tins or you can buy them in accessory packs. Look for a metal muffin tin that fits into your air fryer basket. (I find that metal is more stable than the silicone alternative.)

- **MINI LOAF PANS:** At 5¾ by 3 inches, mini loaf pans are perfect for the air fryer. You can purchase them in sets of three.

- **MEAT THERMOMETER:** I highly recommend that all air fryer owners purchase a dial or digital meat thermometer because all air fryers cook at different rates, and you can get seriously ill by eating undercooked meat.

- **SILICONE OVEN MITTS:** Easily found online, silicone oven mitts are great for removing hot pans from your air fryer.

- **TONGS:** Tongs are especially useful for flipping food during cooking and for getting hot food out of the basket when it is ready to eat.

NICE TO HAVE

- **SILICONE DOUGHNUT MOLDS:** These are perfect for those days when you want to make homemade doughnuts.

- **TOAST RACK:** A toast rack holds toast slices vertically, so you can cook multiple pieces of toast at the same time.

- **MINI CAKE PAN:** You can find cake pans in a variety of smaller sizes (from 4 to 8 inches in diameter) to fit your air fryer.

- **GRILL PAN:** Availability depends on your model, but if you can find a grill pan that fits your air fryer basket, then grab it. It is fabulous for meats.

- **SMALL BUNDT PAN:** Bundt cakes are perfect in the air fryer, because you don't have to worry about the middle cooking. You can find very nice 4-inch Bundt pans and pans up to a 6-cup capacity that fit most air fryers. Check the diameter of your air fryer basket to make sure the pan you choose will fit inside.

ABOUT THE RECIPES

The recipes that follow are all the most common ones that beginners look for. The majority of these recipes require only a few ingredients—mostly fewer than eight items—and they are all common, affordable ingredients that you can find at your local grocery store.

When I developed these recipes, I used a 5.8-quart air fryer. So, most of the recipes were created to serve two to six people. Many recipes can easily be cut in half if you are feeding fewer people.

The recipes will help you understand how to cook in your air fryer and will give you a variety of different foods that you can cook—from muffins and cookies to chicken and steak.

For your reference, each recipe has one or more of the following labels:

- **FAMILY FAVORITE:** These recipes serve at least four people and are kid-friendly, so the whole family can enjoy them.

- **FAST:** These recipes can be made, start to finish, in fewer than 15 minutes.

- **GLUTEN-FREE:** These recipes do not contain any gluten products (but remember to check packages, as some products can be processed in facilities that also process gluten products and can be subject to cross-contamination, which should be noted on the label).

- **VEGAN:** These recipes contain no animal products. They have no meat, poultry, seafood, milk, cheese, or eggs.

- **VEGETARIAN:** These recipes contain no meat, poultry, or seafood.

This cookbook was designed to give you ample exposure to many ways that your air fryer can be used, whether frying, grilling, roasting, baking, or steaming, so each recipe also includes the function that is used for the recipe.

On the following pages is a convenient table that gives time and temperature guidelines for cooking common fresh and frozen foods in your air fryer.

AIR FRYER COOKING CHARTS: FRESH AND FROZEN FOOD

FAVORITE FROZEN FOOD COOKING CHART

FROZEN FOOD	QUANTITY	TIME	TEMPERATURE	NOTES
Breaded shrimp	Up to 1 pound	8 to 10 minutes	400°F	Spray with oil and flip halfway through cooking
Burgers	¼ to 1 pound	14 to 15 minutes	400°F	Do not stack; flip halfway through cooking
Burritos	2 burritos	8 to 10 minutes	400°F	Spray with oil and flip halfway through cooking
Chicken nuggets	1 to 4 cups	10 to 15 minutes	400°F	Spray with oil and shake halfway through cooking
Egg rolls	6 to 8 egg rolls	3 to 6 minutes	390°F	Spray with oil
Fish fillets	¼ to 1 pound	14 to 15 minutes	400°F	Spray with oil and flip halfway through cooking
Fish sticks	¼ to 1 pound	6 to 10 minutes	400°F	Spray with oil and shake halfway through cooking
Hash browns	1 to 2 cups	15 to 18 minutes	370°F	Spray with oil and shake halfway through cooking
Meatballs	Up to 25 meatballs	8 to 10 minutes	380°F	Flip halfway through cooking
Mozzarella sticks	¼ to 1 pound	8 to 10 minutes	360°F	Spray with oil and flip halfway through cooking
Onion rings	1 pound	8 to 10 minutes	400°F	Spray with oil and flip halfway through cooking

FROZEN FOOD	QUANTITY	TIME	TEMPERATURE	NOTES
Pizza	1 pizza	5 to 10 minutes	390°F	Place pizza on parchment paper; make sure it fits in the basket
Pizza bagels	4 or 5 pizza bagels	8 to 10 minutes	375°F	Spray with oil; do not stack
Pizza rolls (bites)	10 pizza rolls	5 to 7 minutes	375°F	Spray with oil and shake halfway through cooking
Pot stickers	1 to 3 cups	8 to 10 minutes	400°F	Spray with oil and flip halfway through cooking
Samosas	6 to 8 samosas	5 to 10 minutes	400°F	Spray with oil and shake halfway through cooking
Tater tots	1¼ to 3 cups	10 to 12 minutes	400°F	Spray with oil and shake halfway through cooking
Thick fries	1¼ to 3 cups	18 to 20 minutes	400°F	Spray with oil and shake halfway through cooking
Thin fries	1¼ to 3 cups	14 minutes	400°F	Spray with oil and shake halfway through cooking

FRESH FOOD COOKING CHART

FRESH VEGETABLES	QUANTITY	TIME	TEMPERATURE	NOTES
Asparagus	1 pound	5 to 8 minutes	400°F	Trim the ends first
Broccoli	2 to 4 cups	5 to 8 minutes	400°F	Season with salt and pepper; spray with oil
Brussels sprouts	2 cups	13 to 15 minutes	380°F	Cut in half lengthwise first; coat with oil and seasonings
Carrots	1 to 2 cups	7 to 10 minutes	380°F	Cut first
Cauliflower florets	2 to 4 cups	9 to 10 minutes	360°F	Coat with oil and seasonings
Corn on the cob	4 ears	6 minutes	390°F	Coat with oil and seasonings
Eggplant	1 to 3 pounds	13 to 15 minutes	400°F	Spray with oil and flip halfway through cooking
Green beans	1 to 3 pounds	5 minutes	400°F	Spray with oil and shake halfway through cooking
Kale	1 bunch	10 to 12 minutes	275°F	Trim leaves from ribs; coat with oil and seasonings
Mushrooms	1 to 2 cups	5 to 8 minutes	400°F	Trim stems first
Onions	1 to 3 pounds	5 to 8 minutes	370°F	Chop first
Peppers (bell)	1 to 2 cups	6 to 8 minutes	370°F	Cut into strips first
Potatoes (baked)	3 or 4 potatoes	40 minutes	400°F	Poke holes or cut slits along the top first

FRESH VEGETABLES	QUANTITY	TIME	TEMPERATURE	NOTES
Potatoes (cubed)	1¼ to 3 cups	15 minutes	400°F	Spray with oil and shake halfway through cooking
Potatoes (fries)	1¼ to 3 cups	15 minutes	380°F	Spray with oil and shake halfway through cooking
Potatoes (wedges)	2 to 4 cups	18 to 20 minutes	380°F	Spray with oil and shake halfway through cooking
Squash	1 pound	12 to 13 minutes	400°F	Coat with oil and seasonings
Sweet potatoes (baked)	2 sweet potatoes	35 to 40 minutes	390°F	Poke holes or cut a slit through the top of each potato first
Sweet potatoes (cubed)	3 to 5 cups	14 to 20 minutes	380°F	Spray with oil and shake halfway through cooking
Sweet potatoes (fries)	1¼ to 3 cups	25 minutes	380°F	Spray with oil and shake halfway through cooking
Tomatoes (breaded)	1 to 3 pounds	10 minutes	350°F	Cut first and apply breading
Zucchini	1 to 3 pounds	10 to 12 minutes	370°F	Cut first

CHICKEN	QUANTITY	TIME	TEMPERATURE	NOTES
Chicken breasts (boneless, skinless)	Up to 4 (6-ounce) breasts	12 to 15 minutes	380°F	Spray with oil and flip halfway through cooking
Chicken drumettes	Up to 8 drumettes	20 minutes	400°F	Spray with oil and shake halfway through cooking
Chicken drumsticks	Up to 6 drumsticks	16 to 20 minutes	390°F	Spray with oil and shake halfway through cooking
Chicken tenders	Up to 8 tenders	8 to 10 minutes	375°F	Spray with oil and shake halfway through cooking
Chicken thighs (bone-in)	Up to 4 (6-ounce) thighs	22 minutes	380°F	Spray with oil and shake halfway through cooking
Chicken thighs (boneless)	Up to 4 (6-ounce) thighs	18 to 20 minutes	380°F	Spray with oil and shake halfway through cooking
Chicken wings	Up to 8 wings	15 to 20 minutes	400°F	Spray with oil and shake halfway through cooking
Whole chicken	2 pounds	75 minutes	360°F	Coat with oil and seasonings

BEEF	QUANTITY	TIME	TEMPERATURE	NOTES
Burgers	¼ to 1 pound	8 to 10 minutes	400°F	Do not stack; flip halfway through cooking
Filet mignon	Up to 4 (6-ounce) steaks	8 to 10 minutes	360°F	Time will vary depending on desired doneness; use a meat thermometer and cook to 125°F for rare, 135°F for medium-rare, 145°F for medium, 155°F for medium-well, and 160°F for well-done
Flank steak	¼ to 1 pound	8 to 10 minutes	360°F	Time will vary depending on desired doneness; use a meat thermometer and cook to 125°F for rare, 135°F for medium-rare, 145°F for medium, 155°F for medium-well, and 160°F for well-done
Meatballs	Up to 25 meatballs	7 to 10 minutes	380°F	Flip halfway through cooking
Rib eye steak	Up to 4 (6-ounce) steaks	10 to 15 minutes	380°F	Time will vary depending on desired doneness; use a meat thermometer and cook to 125°F for rare, 135°F for medium-rare, 145°F for medium, 155°F for medium-well, and 160°F for well-done
Sirloin steak	Up to 4 (6-ounce) steaks	12 to 14 minutes	400°F	Time will vary depending on desired doneness; use a meat thermometer and cook to 125°F for rare, 135°F for medium-rare, 145°F for medium, 155°F for medium-well, and 160°F for well-done

PORK AND LAMB	QUANTITY	TIME	TEMPERATURE	NOTES
Bacon	6 slices	7 to 10 minutes	400°F	Flip halfway through cooking
Lamb chops	¼ to 1 pound	10 to 12 minutes	400°F	Do not stack; flip halfway through cooking
Pork chops (bone-in or boneless)	¼ to 1 pound	12 to 15 minutes	380°F	Spray with oil and flip halfway cooking
Pork loin	¼ to 1 pound	50 to 60 minutes	360°F	Sprinkle with seasonings and flip halfway through cooking
Pork tenderloin	¼ to 1 pound	12 to 15 minutes	390°F	Drizzle with oil and cook whole
Rack of lamb	¼ to 1 pound	22 to 25 minutes	380°F	Do not stack; flip halfway through cooking
Sausage (links)	¼ to 1 pound	13 to 15 minutes	380°F	Pierce holes in sausages first
Sausage (patties)	Up to 6 patties	13 to 15 minutes	380°F	Flip halfway through cooking

FISH AND SEAFOOD	QUANTITY	TIME	TEMPERATURE	NOTES
Crab cakes	4 crab cakes	8 to 10 minutes	375°F	Toss with all-purpose flour and coat with oil
Fish fillets	¼ to 1 pound	10 to 12 minutes	320°F	Coat with oil and seasonings
Scallops	¼ to 1 pound	5 to 7 minutes	320°F	Coat with oil and sprinkle with seasonings
Shrimp	¼ to 1 pound	7 to 8 minutes	400°F	Peel and devein; coat with oil and seasonings

FRESH FRUIT	QUANTITY	TIME	TEMPERATURE	NOTES
Apples	2 to 4 cups	4 to 7 minutes	350°F	Cut first
Bananas	2 to 4 cups	4 to 7 minutes	350°F	Cut first
Peaches	2 to 4 cups	5 to 6 minutes	350°F	Cut first

BREAKFAST

< Air Fryer Homemade Blueberry Muffins,
page 33

AIR FRYER HARD-BOILED EGGS

FAMILY FAVORITE, GLUTEN-FREE, VEGETARIAN

This is the greatest air fryer hack—hard-boiled eggs without the boiling water! What could be simpler? I make a batch every Sunday, so we can have a quick breakfast or an on-the-go snack. It is absolutely the easiest way to make hard-boiled eggs for any purpose, from snacking to egg salad to potato salad. For the beginner, this is a great way to experiment with the air fryer.

BAKE / 250°F

PREP TIME: 1 MINUTE

COOK TIME: 15 MINUTES

SERVES 6

———

6 eggs

1. Place the eggs in the air fryer basket. (You can put the eggs in an oven-safe bowl if you are worried about them rolling around and breaking.)

2. Set the temperature to 250°F. Set the timer and bake for 15 minutes (if you prefer a soft-boiled egg, reduce the cook time to 10 minutes).

3. Meanwhile, fill a medium mixing bowl half full of ice water.

4. Use tongs to remove the eggs from the air fryer basket, and transfer them to the ice water bath.

5. Let the eggs sit for 5 minutes in the ice water.

6. Peel and eat on the spot or refrigerate for up to 1 week.

INGREDIENT TIP: A great way to peel hard-boiled eggs is to first crack the shell on a hard surface and then roll them in the palms of your hands. The shell should come off easily.

Per Serving: Calories: 72; Fat: 5g; Saturated fat: 2g; Carbohydrate: 0g; Fiber: 0g; Sugar: 0g; Protein: 6g; Iron: 1mg; Sodium: 70mg

EASY AIR FRYER BAKED EGGS WITH CHEESE

FAST, GLUTEN-FREE, VEGETARIAN

This is a great way to prepare eggs in the air fryer. You can reduce the cook time for a softer yolk—what my kids call "dunkie eggs," which are great served with toast fingers. You can serve a baked egg on a bagel, toast, or English muffin, along with Foolproof Air Fryer Bacon (page 30) for a terrific breakfast sandwich.

BAKE / 330°F

PREP TIME: 2 MINUTES

COOK TIME: 6 MINUTES

SERVES 2

---

2 large eggs

2 tablespoons half-and-half, divided

2 teaspoons shredded Cheddar cheese, divided

Salt

Freshly ground black pepper

1. Lightly coat the insides of 2 (8-ounce) ramekins with cooking spray.

2. Break an egg into each ramekin.

3. Add 1 tablespoon of half-and-half and 1 teaspoon of cheese to each ramekin. Season with salt and pepper.

4. Using a fork, stir the egg mixture.

5. Set the ramekins in the air fryer basket.

6. Set the temperature to 330°F. Set the timer and bake for 6 minutes.

7. Check the eggs to make sure they are cooked. If they are not done, cook for 1 minute more and check again.

8. Using silicone oven mitts, remove the hot ramekins from the air fryer and serve.

VARIATION TIP: Change this up by mixing in some diced vegetables. I've used red bell pepper, green bell pepper, onions, kale, and spinach. You can also change your container: Scoop out the centers of two avocado halves, leaving 1 inch around the edge and on the bottom, then use the avocados as your ramekins.

Per Serving: Calories: 100; Fat: 8g; Saturated fat: 3g; Carbohydrate: 1g; Fiber: 0g; Sugar: 0g; Protein: 7g; Iron: 1mg; Sodium: 168mg

FOOLPROOF AIR FRYER BACON

FAMILY FAVORITE, GLUTEN-FREE

Bacon cooked in the air fryer is the best I've ever had and—in my book—this alone is reason enough to purchase an air fryer. There's no standing over a hot stove or dodging grease spatter flying off a hot griddle. Try this, pronto. You'll never look back.

FRY / 400°F

PREP TIME: 5 MINUTES

COOK TIME: 10 TO 12 MINUTES

SERVES 5

---

10 slices bacon

1. Cut the bacon slices in half, so they will fit in the air fryer.

2. Place the half-slices in the fryer basket in a single layer. (You may need to cook the bacon in more than one batch.)

3. Set the temperature to 400°F. Set the timer and fry for 5 minutes.

4. Open the drawer and check the bacon. (The power of the fan may have caused the bacon to fly around during the cooking process. If so, use a fork or tongs to rearrange the slices.)

5. Reset the timer and fry for 5 minutes more.

6. When the time has elapsed, check the bacon again. If you like your bacon crispier, cook it for another 1 to 2 minutes.

AIR FRYER TIP: If you have a hard time with the bacon moving around a lot during cooking due to the fan, put a metal trivet or a metal rack on top of the bacon slices to keep them in place during the cooking process.

Per Serving: Calories: 87; Fat: 7g; Saturated fat: 2g; Carbohydrate: 0g; Fiber: 0g; Sugar: 0g; Protein: 6g; Iron: 0mg; Sodium: 370mg

EASY AIR FRYER BUTTERMILK BISCUITS

FAMILY FAVORITE, FAST, VEGETARIAN

Biscuits are an easy and delicious breakfast classic. They can be made the night before for a quick grab-and-go breakfast. They also make a great Saturday or Sunday morning breakfast served with homemade sausage gravy.

BAKE / 360°F

PREP TIME: 5 MINUTES

COOK TIME: 5 MINUTES

MAKES 12 BISCUITS

---

2 cups all-purpose flour

1 tablespoon baking powder

¼ teaspoon baking soda

2 teaspoons sugar

1 teaspoon salt

6 tablespoons (¾ stick) cold unsalted butter, cut into 1-tablespoon slices

¾ cup buttermilk

4 tablespoons (½ stick) unsalted butter, melted (optional)

1. Spray the air fryer basket with olive oil.
2. In a large mixing bowl, combine the flour, baking powder, baking soda, sugar, and salt and mix well.
3. Using a fork, cut in the butter until the mixture resembles coarse meal.
4. Add the buttermilk and mix until smooth.
5. Sprinkle flour on a clean work surface. Turn the dough out onto the work surface and roll it out until it is about ½ inch thick.
6. Using a 2-inch biscuit cutter, cut out the biscuits. Place the uncooked biscuits in the greased air fryer basket in a single layer.
7. Set the temperature to 360°F. Set the timer and bake for 5 minutes.
8. Transfer the cooked biscuits from the air fryer to a platter. Brush the tops with melted butter, if desired.
9. Cut the remaining biscuits (you may have to gather up the scraps of dough and reroll the dough for the last couple of biscuits). Bake the remaining biscuits.
10. Plate, serve, and enjoy!

SUBSTITUTION TIP: If you don't have buttermilk on hand, it's easy to make. In a small mixing bowl, mix 1 cup of milk with 1 tablespoon of white vinegar to make 1 cup of buttermilk.

Per Serving (1 biscuit): Calories: 146; Fat: 6g; Saturated fat: 4g; Carbohydrate: 20g; Fiber: 1g; Sugar: 2g; Protein: 3g; Iron: 1mg; Sodium: 280mg

BLUEBERRY PANCAKE POPPERS

FAMILY FAVORITE, FAST, VEGETARIAN

My kids love these. I usually make a batch over the weekend and freeze them, then reheat them as needed in the microwave. I also just pop them in the kids' lunches in the morning, and by lunchtime they are thawed and ready to eat.

BAKE / 320°F

PREP TIME: 5 MINUTES

COOK TIME: 8 MINUTES

MAKES 8 PANCAKE POPPERS

---

1 cup all-purpose flour

1 tablespoon sugar

1 teaspoon baking soda

½ teaspoon baking powder

1 cup milk

1 large egg

1 teaspoon vanilla extract

1 teaspoon olive oil

½ cup fresh blueberries

1. In a medium mixing bowl, combine the flour, sugar, baking soda, and baking powder and mix well.

2. Mix in the milk, egg, vanilla, and oil.

3. Coat the inside of an air fryer muffin tin with cooking spray.

4. Fill each muffin cup two-thirds full. (You may have to bake the poppers in more than one batch.)

5. Drop a few blueberries into each muffin cup.

6. Set the muffin tin into the air fryer basket.

7. Set the temperature to 320°F. Set the timer and bake for 8 minutes.

8. Insert a toothpick into the center of a pancake popper; if it comes out clean, they are done. If batter clings to the toothpick, cook the poppers for 2 minutes more and check again.

9. When the poppers are cooked through, use silicone oven mitts to remove the muffin tin from the air fryer basket. Turn out the poppers onto a wire rack to cool.

SUBSTITUTION TIP: Try these with chocolate chips, bacon bits, or bite-size sausage pieces instead of blueberries. Top with some fresh maple syrup.

Per Serving (1 popper): Calories: 103; Fat: 2g; Saturated fat: 1g; Carbohydrate: 18g; Fiber: 1g; Sugar: 4g; Protein: 4g; Iron: 1mg; Sodium: 181mg

AIR FRYER HOMEMADE BLUEBERRY MUFFINS

FAMILY FAVORITE, VEGETARIAN

This is a great, healthy breakfast to grab when you're on the go. These muffins can be made ahead of time, but the blueberries coming right out of the air fryer have a great flavor, so they are best eaten warm.

BAKE / 320°F

PREP TIME: 5 MINUTES

COOK TIME: 14 MINUTES

SERVES 10

⅔ cup all-purpose flour

1 teaspoon baking powder

2 tablespoons sugar

1 egg

2 teaspoons vanilla extract

⅓ cup low-fat milk

3 tablespoons unsalted butter, melted

¾ cup fresh blueberries

1. In a medium mixing bowl, combine the flour, baking powder, sugar, egg, vanilla, milk, and melted butter and mix well.
2. Fold in the blueberries.
3. Coat the inside of an air fryer muffin tin with cooking spray.
4. Fill each muffin cup about two-thirds full.
5. Set the muffin tin into the air fryer basket. (You may need to cook the muffins in more than one batch.)
6. Set the temperature to 320°F. Set the timer and bake for 14 minutes.
7. Insert a toothpick into the center of a muffin; if it comes out clean, they are done. If batter clings to the toothpick, cook the muffins for 2 minutes more and check again.
8. When the muffins are cooked through, use silicone oven mitts to remove the muffin tin from the air fryer basket. Turn out the muffins onto a wire rack to cool slightly before serving.

AIR FRYER TIP: Look for special-size muffin tins for the air fryer. They can be found individually or in air fryer accessory kits in the kitchen department of large department stores or online.

Per Serving: Calories: 92; Fat: 4g; Saturated fat: 2g; Carbohydrate: 12g; Fiber: 1g; Sugar: 4g; Protein: 2g; Iron: 1mg; Sodium: 35mg

HOMEMADE AIR FRIED BANANA BREAD

FAMILY FAVORITE, VEGETARIAN

Sweet, moist, and comforting, this banana bread can be made in fewer than 30 minutes and tastes amazing straight out of the air fryer. It is a staple at our house: I often bake a batch on Sunday night, so the kids have something healthy and delicious to take to school. As an added bonus, it makes your kitchen smell wonderful.

BAKE / 310°F

PREP TIME: 5 MINUTES

COOK TIME: 22 MINUTES

MAKES 3 (5.75-INCH-BY-3.25-INCH) LOAVES

---

3 ripe bananas, mashed

1 cup sugar

1 large egg

4 tablespoons (½ stick) unsalted butter, melted

1½ cups all-purpose flour

1 teaspoon baking soda

1 teaspoon salt

1. Coat the insides of 3 mini loaf pans with cooking spray.
2. In a large mixing bowl, mix together the bananas and sugar.
3. In a separate large mixing bowl, combine the egg, butter, flour, baking soda, and salt and mix well.
4. Add the banana mixture to the egg and flour mixture. Mix well.
5. Divide the batter evenly among the prepared pans.
6. Set the mini loaf pans into the air fryer basket.
7. Set the temperature to 310°F. Set the timer and bake for 22 minutes.
8. Insert a toothpick into the center of each loaf; if it comes out clean, they are done. If the batter clings to the toothpick, cook the loaves for 2 minutes more and check again.
9. When the loaves are cooked through, use silicone oven mitts to remove the pans from the air fryer basket. Turn out the loaves onto a wire rack to cool.

INGREDIENT TIP: For sweet banana bread, wait until the bananas are almost black. Overripe bananas make your banana bread moist and give it an extra boost of banana flavor.

Per Serving (½ loaf): Calories: 256; Fat: 6g; Saturated fat: 4g; Carbohydrate: 49g; Fiber: 2g; Sugar: 27g; Protein: 4g; Iron: 1mg; Sodium: 444mg

AIR FRYER CINNAMON ROLLS

FAMILY FAVORITE, VEGETARIAN

This is the first thing I cooked in my air fryer. They come out absolutely light, fluffy, and just plain delicious. My kids love when I make them. With a hot cup of coffee and the morning paper, these are a perfect Sunday morning breakfast food.

BAKE / 340° F

PREP TIME: 5 MINUTES

COOK TIME: 12 MINUTES

MAKES 8 CINNAMON ROLLS

---

1 can of cinnamon rolls

1. Spray the air fryer basket with olive oil.
2. Separate the canned cinnamon rolls and place them in the air fryer basket.
3. Set the temperature to 340°F. Set the timer and bake for 6 minutes.
4. Using tongs, flip the cinnamon rolls. Reset the timer and bake for another 6 minutes.
5. When the rolls are done cooking, use tongs to remove them from the air fryer. Transfer them to a platter and spread them with the icing that comes in the package.

AIR FRYER TIP: While grocery shopping, keep an eye out for prepared items that work in your air fryer (see the Fresh and Frozen Food Cooking Charts on page 18). When you are short on time, it's great to have something delicious to eat that can be ready in minutes.

Per Serving: Calories: 145; Fat: 5g; Saturated fat: 2g; Carbohydrate: 23g; Fiber: 1g; Sugar: 10g; Protein: 2g; Iron: 1mg; Sodium: 340mg

SNACKS AND APPETIZERS

< Parmesan Dill Fried Pickles,
 page 48

RANCH ROASTED CHICKPEAS

FAMILY FAVORITE, FAST, GLUTEN-FREE, VEGAN

This is a great protein-rich snack. Eat them as they are, or use them on top of salads, soup, or even your favorite chicken dish. They are a great add-on to most meals.

ROAST / 350°F

PREP TIME: 4 MINUTES

COOK TIME: 10 MINUTES

SERVES 4

---

1 (15-ounce) can chickpeas, drained and rinsed

1 tablespoon olive oil

3 tablespoons ranch seasoning mix

1 teaspoon salt

2 tablespoons freshly squeezed lemon juice

1. Spray the air fryer basket with olive oil.

2. Using paper towels, pat the chickpeas dry.

3. In a medium mixing bowl, mix together the chickpeas, oil, seasoning mix, salt, and lemon juice.

4. Put the chickpeas in the air fryer basket and spread them out in a single layer. (You may need to cook the chickpeas in more than one batch.)

5. Set the temperature to 350°F. Set the timer and roast for 4 minutes. Remove the drawer and shake vigorously to redistribute the chickpeas so they cook evenly. Reset the timer and roast for 6 minutes more.

6. When the time is up, release the air fryer basket from the drawer and pour the chickpeas into a bowl. Season with additional salt, if desired. Enjoy!

SUBSTITUTION TIP: Try a different seasoning. If you like Cajun, for example, substitute a Cajun mix for the ranch seasoning.

Per Serving: Calories: 144; Fat: 5g; Saturated fat: 1g; Carbohydrate: 19g; Fiber: 5g; Sugar: 3g; Protein: 6g; Iron: 2mg; Sodium: 891mg

HOMEMADE AIR FRYER ROASTED MIXED NUTS

FAMILY FAVORITE, GLUTEN-FREE, VEGETARIAN

The hardest part about making this appetizer for a crowd is waiting for everyone to arrive before you start eating. These nuts are too easy to eat right out of the air fryer. The cinnamon, paprika, and sugar add a spicy sweetness that is absolutely wonderful. Preheating the air fryer is crucial for this recipe; just remember that the air fryer basket will be hot, so do not touch it.

ROAST / 300°F

PREP TIME: 5 MINUTES

COOK TIME: 20 MINUTES

SERVES 6

2 cups mixed nuts (walnuts, pecans, and/or almonds)

2 tablespoons egg white

1 teaspoon ground cinnamon

2 tablespoons sugar

1 teaspoon paprika

1. Preheat the air fryer to 300°F and spray the air fryer basket with olive oil.

2. In a small mixing bowl, mix together the nuts, egg white, cinnamon, sugar, and paprika, until the nuts are thoroughly coated.

3. Place the nuts in the greased air fryer basket; set the timer and roast for 10 minutes.

4. After 10 minutes, remove the drawer and shake the basket to redistribute the nuts so they roast evenly. Reset the timer and roast for 10 minutes more.

5. Release the basket from the drawer, pour the nuts into a bowl, and serve.

SUBSTITUTION TIP: A great way to alter this recipe is to play with the spices. Try substituting 2 tablespoons of fresh rosemary, 1 tablespoon of brown sugar, 1 teaspoon of ground cumin, 1 teaspoon of salt, and 2 tablespoons of maple sugar for the cinnamon, sugar, and paprika.

Per Serving: Calories: 232; Fat: 21g; Saturated fat: 2g; Carbohydrate: 10g; Fiber: 3g; Sugar: 5g; Protein: 6g; Iron: 1mg; Sodium: 6mg

EASY TOMATO AND BASIL BRUSCHETTA

FAMILY FAVORITE, FAST, VEGETARIAN

Bruschetta is one of my family's favorite recipes. It is amazing in the summer months when the tomatoes are vine-ripened and the basil is freshly picked. As a bonus, bruschetta is incredibly easy to make and the air fryer toasts the bread perfectly.

TOAST / 250°F

PREP TIME: 5 MINUTES

COOK TIME: 3 MINUTES

SERVES 6

---

4 tomatoes, diced

⅓ cup fresh basil, shredded

¼ cup shredded Parmesan cheese

1 tablespoon minced garlic

1 tablespoon balsamic vinegar

1 teaspoon olive oil

1 teaspoon salt

1 teaspoon freshly ground black pepper

1 loaf French bread

1. In a medium mixing bowl, combine the tomatoes and basil.
2. Mix in the Parmesan cheese, garlic, vinegar, olive oil, salt, and pepper.
3. Let the tomato mixture sit and marinate, while you prepare the bread.
4. Spray the air fryer basket with olive oil.
5. Cut the bread into 1-inch-thick slices.
6. Place the slices in the greased air fryer basket in a single layer. (You may have to toast the bread in more than one batch.)
7. Spray the top of the bread with olive oil.
8. Set the temperature to 250°F. Set the timer and toast for 3 minutes.
9. Using tongs, remove the bread slices from the air fryer and place a spoonful of the bruschetta topping on each piece.

AIR FRYER TIP: Toasting bread in the air fryer is best done on low temperature, and there always needs to be a coating on the bread; otherwise, when the bread comes in contact with the heat, it will dry out. So, to keep your bread toasted on the outside but soft on the inside, don't forget to use olive oil or another fat when toasting it in the air fryer.

Per Serving: Calories: 258; Fat: 3g; Saturated fat: 1g; Carbohydrate: 47g; Fiber: 3g; Sugar: 4g; Protein: 11g; Iron: 3mg; Sodium: 826mg

"EVERYTHING" SEASONED SAUSAGE ROLLS

FAMILY FAVORITE, FAST

Whether it's game time or a quick afternoon snack for the kids, this twist on the classic pigs in a blanket is always a hit. Using prepared crescent rolls is a great shortcut to get these on the table in a matter of minutes. Serve with ketchup and mustard for dipping.

BAKE / 330°F

PREP TIME: 5 MINUTES

COOK TIME: 5 MINUTES

SERVES 6

___

FOR THE SEASONING

2 tablespoons sesame seeds

1½ teaspoons poppy seeds

1½ teaspoons dried minced onion

1 teaspoon salt

1 teaspoon dried minced garlic

FOR THE SAUSAGES

1 (8-ounce) package crescent roll dough

1 (12-ounce) package mini smoked sausages (cocktail franks)

TO MAKE THE SEASONING

In a small bowl, combine the sesame seeds, poppy seeds, onion, salt, and garlic and set aside.

TO MAKE THE SAUSAGES

1. Spray the air fryer basket with olive oil.
2. Remove the crescent dough from the package and lay it out on a cutting board. Separate the dough at the perforations. Using a pizza cutter or sharp knife, cut each triangle of dough into fourths.
3. Drain the sausages and pat them dry with a paper towel.
4. Roll each sausage in a piece of dough.
5. Sprinkle seasoning on top of each roll.
6. Place the seasoned sausage rolls into the greased air fryer basket in a single layer. (You will have to bake these in at least 2 batches.)
7. Set the temperature to 330°F. Set the timer for 5 minutes.
8. Using tongs, remove the sausages from the air fryer and place them on a platter.
9. Repeat steps 6 through 8 with the second batch.

___

SUBSTITUTION TIP: Leave off the seasoning and try this recipe with breakfast sausage for a quick and fun breakfast.

___

Per Serving: Calories: 344; Fat: 26g; Saturated fat: 8g; Carbohydrate: 17g; Fiber: 1g; Sugar: 3g; Protein: 10g; Iron: 2mg; Sodium: 1145mg

EASY MOZZARELLA STICKS

This is one of the easiest recipes you will find for homemade mozzarella sticks, as they do not require freezing time. I usually serve mine along with a dish of hot marinara sauce for dipping.

BAKE / 370°F

PREP TIME: 10 MINUTES

COOK TIME: 8 MINUTES

SERVES 6

---

1 (12-count) package mozzarella sticks

1 (8-ounce) package crescent roll dough

3 tablespoons unsalted butter, melted

¼ cup panko bread crumbs

Marinara sauce, for dipping (optional)

1. Spray the air fryer basket with olive oil.
2. Cut each cheese stick into thirds.
3. Unroll the crescent roll dough. Using a pizza cutter or sharp knife, cut the dough into 36 even pieces.
4. Wrap each small cheese stick in a piece of dough. Make sure that the dough is wrapped tightly around the cheese. Pinch the dough together at both ends, and pinch along the seam to ensure that the dough is completely sealed.
5. Using tongs, dip the wrapped cheese sticks in the melted butter, then dip the cheese sticks in the panko bread crumbs.
6. Place the cheese sticks in the greased air fryer basket in a single layer. (You may have to cook the cheese sticks in more than one batch.)
7. Set the temperature to 370°F. Set the timer and bake for 5 minutes. After 5 minutes, the tops should be golden brown.
8. Using tongs, flip the cheese sticks and bake for another 3 minutes, or until golden brown on all sides.
9. Repeat until you use all of the dough.
10. Plate, serve with the marinara sauce (if you like), and enjoy!

COOKING TIP: The key to this recipe is to make sure that the dough is tightly wrapped around the cheese so that it does not become loose during cooking.

Per Serving: Calories: 348; Fat: 23g; Saturated fat: 13g; Carbohydrate: 21g; Fiber: 1g; Sugar: 3g; Protein: 17g; Iron: 1mg; Sodium: 811mg

HOMEMADE AIR FRYER PITA CHIPS

FAMILY FAVORITE, FAST, VEGAN

Make these fast and flavorful homemade pita chips to serve along with your favorite appetizer or dip. I usually make a huge batch on Sunday and place them in small containers for the kids to take to school for lunch, along with a small container of hummus for dipping.

BAKE / 350°F

PREP TIME: 5 MINUTES

COOK TIME: 6 MINUTES

SERVES 4

---

2 pieces whole wheat pita bread

3 tablespoons olive oil

1 teaspoon freshly squeezed lemon juice

1 teaspoon salt

1 teaspoon dried basil

1 teaspoon garlic powder

1. Spray the air fryer basket with olive oil.

2. Using a pair of kitchen shears or a pizza cutter, cut the pita bread into small wedges.

3. Place the wedges in a small mixing bowl and add the olive oil, lemon juice, salt, dried basil, and garlic powder.

4. Mix well, coating each wedge.

5. Place the seasoned pita wedges in the greased air fryer basket in a single layer, being careful not to overcrowd them. (You may have to bake the pita chips in more than one batch.)

6. Set the temperature to 350°F. Set the timer and bake for 6 minutes. Every 2 minutes or so, remove the drawer and shake the pita chips so they redistribute in the basket for even cooking.

7. Serve with your choice of dip or alone as a tasty snack.

SUBSTITUTION TIP: To make homemade cinnamon-sugar pita chips, replace the lemon juice, salt, dried basil, and garlic powder with ¼ cup of olive oil, 4 teaspoons of sugar, and 1 teaspoon of ground cinnamon.

Per Serving: Calories: 178; Fat: 11g; Saturated fat: 2g; Carbohydrate: 18g; Fiber: 3g; Sugar: 1g; Protein: 3g; Iron: 1mg; Sodium: 752mg

HEALTHY CARROT CHIPS

FAMILY FAVORITE, FAST, GLUTEN-FREE, VEGAN

These are a healthy alternative to regular potato chips. They are also keto and Whole30 compliant. So, if you are having a party and want something that everyone can eat, this is the recipe for you. Serve them hot, accompanied by a creamy dip.

BAKE / 360°F

PREP TIME: 5 MINUTES

COOK TIME: 6 TO 8 MINUTES

SERVES 6

---

1 pound carrots, peeled and sliced ⅛ inch thick

2 tablespoons olive oil

1 teaspoon sea salt

1. In a large mixing bowl, combine the carrots, olive oil, and salt. Toss them together until the carrot slices are thoroughly coated with oil.

2. Place the carrot chips in the air fryer basket in a single layer. (You may have to bake the carrot chips in more than one batch.)

3. Set the temperature to 360°F. Set the timer and bake for 3 minutes. Remove the air fryer drawer and shake to redistribute the chips for even cooking. Reset the timer and bake for 3 minutes more.

4. Check the carrot chips for doneness. If you like them extra crispy, give the basket another shake and cook them for another 1 to 2 minutes.

5. When the chips are done, release the air fryer basket from the drawer, pour the chips into a bowl, and serve.

SUBSTITUTION TIP: Feel free to replace the carrots with any other type of fruit or vegetable (cooking times may vary slightly). I've tried kale chips, apple chips, and root vegetable chips. All are delicious, kid-friendly, and healthy snacks.

Per Serving: Calories: 71; Fat: 5g; Saturated fat: 1g; Carbohydrate: 7g; Fiber: 2g; Sugar: 4g; Protein: 1g; Iron: 0mg; Sodium: 364mg

AIR FRIED HOMEMADE POTATO CHIPS

FAMILY-FAVORITE, GLUTEN-FREE, VEGAN

How many people can say they have made their own potato chips? This is a great recipe to make with kids. But be forewarned: They may end up eating their weight in potato chips. These are best served straight from the air fryer, sprinkled with sea salt.

FRY / 375°F

PREP TIME: 5 MINUTES

COOK TIME: 15 TO 25 MINUTES

SERVES 4

---

4 yellow potatoes

1 tablespoon olive oil

1 tablespoon salt
(plus more for topping)

1. Using a mandoline or sharp knife, slice the potatoes into ⅛-inch-thick slices.

2. In a medium mixing bowl, toss the potato slices with the olive oil and salt until the potatoes are thoroughly coated with oil.

3. Place the potatoes in the air fryer basket in a single layer. (You may have to fry the potato chips in more than one batch.)

4. Set the temperature to 375°F. Set the timer and fry for 15 minutes.

5. Shake the basket several times during cooking, so the chips crisp evenly and don't burn.

6. Check to see if they are fork-tender; if not, add another 5 to 10 minutes, checking frequently. They will crisp up after they are removed from the air fryer.

7. Season with additional salt, if desired.

VARIATION TIP: This is a great recipe for a starter; you can add to it and change it in many ways. To make barbecue potato chips, combine 1 tablespoon of garlic powder, 1 tablespoon of onion powder, 1 tablespoon of brown sugar, ½ teaspoon of paprika, ½ teaspoon of salt, and a pinch of cayenne pepper. Add the seasonings after the potato chips are cooked.

Per Serving: Calories: 177; Fat: 4g; Saturated fat: 1g; Carbohydrate: 34g; Fiber: 5g; Sugar: 3g; Protein: 4g; Iron: 1mg; Sodium: 1757mg

LOADED POTATO SKINS

FAMILY FAVORITE, GLUTEN-FREE

A classic appetizer that can be made in a flash, these potato skins are great for every occasion—football parties, potlucks, or a family game night. You can even set up a potato bar and everyone in the family can load up their own before you pop them in the air fryer.

BAKE / 400°F

PREP TIME: 10 MINUTES

COOK TIME: 12 MINUTES

SERVES 4

———

4 medium russet potatoes, baked

Olive oil

Salt

Freshly ground black pepper

2 cups shredded Cheddar cheese

4 slices cooked bacon, chopped

Finely chopped scallions, for topping

Sour cream, for topping

Finely chopped olives, for topping

1. Spray the air fryer basket with oil.

2. Cut each baked potato in half.

3. Using a large spoon, scoop out the center of each potato half, leaving about 1 inch of the potato flesh around the edges and the bottom.

4. Rub olive oil over the inside of each baked potato half and season with salt and pepper, then place the potato skins in the greased air fryer basket.

5. Set the temperature to 400°F. Set the timer and bake for 10 minutes.

6. After 10 minutes, remove the potato skins and fill them with the shredded Cheddar cheese and bacon, then bake in the air fryer for another 2 minutes, just until the cheese is melted.

7. Garnish the potato skins with the scallions, sour cream, and olives.

COOKING TIP: You can bake these potatoes in the air fryer. Set the temperature to 400° F and cook the potatoes for 40 to 50 minutes, or until fork tender.

Per Serving: Calories: 487; Fat: 31g; Saturated fat: 16g; Carbohydrate: 29g; Fiber: 5g; Sugar: 1g; Protein: 24g; Iron: 5mg; Sodium: 986mg

FRESH HOMEMADE POTATO WEDGES

FAMILY FAVORITE, GLUTEN-FREE, VEGAN

This is a great way to use up potatoes and have an awesome starter for everyone to enjoy. These fresh-cut potatoes are roasted in the air fryer with a pinch of paprika for a smoky, spicy flavor. Feel free to substitute your own favorite herbs and spices for the paprika to make it your own.

ROAST / 400°F

PREP TIME: 5 MINUTES

COOK TIME: 20 TO 25 MINUTES

SERVES 4

4 russet potatoes

2 teaspoons salt, divided

1 teaspoon freshly ground black pepper

1 teaspoon paprika

1 to 3 tablespoons olive oil, divided

1. Cut the potatoes into ½-inch-thick wedges. Try to make the wedges uniform in size, so they cook at an even rate.

2. In a medium mixing bowl, combine the potato wedges with 1 teaspoon of salt, pepper, paprika, and 1 tablespoon of olive oil. Toss until all the potatoes are thoroughly coated with oil. Add additional oil, if needed.

3. Place the potato wedges in the air fryer basket in a single layer. (You may have to roast them in batches.)

4. Set the temperature to 400°F. Set the timer and roast for 5 minutes.

5. After 5 minutes, remove the air fryer drawer and shake the potatoes to keep them from sticking. Reset the timer and roast the potatoes for another 5 minutes, then shake again. Repeat this process until the potatoes have cooked for a total of 20 minutes.

6. Check and see if the potatoes are cooked. If they are not fork-tender, roast for 5 minutes more.

7. Using tongs, remove the potato wedges from the air fryer basket and transfer them to a bowl. Toss with the remaining salt.

SUBSTITUTION TIP: This is a great recipe for sweet potato wedges—simply use sweet potatoes instead of russet potatoes and follow the recipe as instructed.

Per Serving: Calories: 210; Fat: 7g; Saturated fat: 1g; Carbohydrate: 34g; Fiber: 6g; Sugar: 3g; Protein: 4g; Iron: 1mg; Sodium: 1176mg

PARMESAN DILL FRIED PICKLES

FAMILY FAVORITE, VEGETARIAN

Before the air fryer, the place to get fried pickles was at the fair. Not anymore. Now you can have delicious fried pickles at home, in a matter of minutes! Use dill pickles that are sliced in chips (or discs), and not sandwich dills that are sliced lengthwise.

FRY / 390°F

PREP TIME: 5 MINUTES, PLUS 20 MINUTES TO DRY

COOK TIME: 4 MINUTES

SERVES 4

---

1 (16-ounce) jar sliced dill pickles

⅔ cup panko bread crumbs

⅓ cup grated Parmesan cheese

¼ teaspoon dried dill

2 large eggs

1. Line a platter with a double thickness of paper towels. Spread the pickles out in a single layer on the paper towels. Let the pickles drain on the towels for 20 minutes. After 20 minutes have passed, pat the pickles again with a clean paper towel to get them as dry as possible before breading.

2. Spray the air fryer basket with olive oil.

3. In a small mixing bowl, combine the panko bread crumbs, Parmesan cheese, and dried dill. Mix well.

4. In a separate small bowl, crack the eggs and beat until frothy.

5. Dip each pickle into the egg mixture, then into the bread crumb mixture. Make sure the pickle is fully coated in breading.

6. Place the breaded pickle slices in the greased air fryer basket in a single layer. (You may have to fry your pickles in more than one batch.)

7. Spray the pickles with a generous amount of olive oil.

8. Set the temperature to 390°F. Set the timer and fry for 4 minutes.

9. Open the air fryer drawer and use tongs to flip the pickles. Spray them again with olive oil. Reset the timer and fry for another 4 minutes.

10. Using tongs, remove the pickles from the drawer. Plate, serve, and enjoy!

VARIATION TIP: For an additional treat, serve the fried pickles with a tangy dipping sauce. Just mix together ½ cup of mayonnaise, 1 tablespoon of ketchup, and 1 teaspoon of Cajun seasoning.

Per Serving: Calories: 153; Fat: 6g; Saturated fat: 3g; Carbohydrate: 16g; Fiber: 2g; Sugar: 3g; Protein: 9g; Iron: 2mg; Sodium: 1634mg

AIR FRYER STUFFED MUSHROOMS

FAMILY FAVORITE, FAST, VEGAN

This is a real crowd-pleaser; everyone loves stuffed mushrooms. This recipe can also be made a day ahead, which saves time when you're entertaining. Stuffed mushrooms cooked in the air fryer have a nice, earthy flavor to them.

BAKE / 360°F

PREP TIME: 5 MINUTES

COOK TIME: 10 MINUTES

SERVES 4

---

12 medium button mushrooms

½ cup bread crumbs

1 teaspoon salt

½ teaspoon freshly ground black pepper

5 to 6 tablespoons olive oil

1. Spray the air fryer basket with olive oil.
2. Separate the cap from the stem of each mushroom. Discard the stems.
3. In a small mixing bowl, combine the bread crumbs, salt, pepper, and olive oil until you have a wet mixture.
4. Rub the mushrooms with olive oil on all sides.
5. Using a spoon, fill each mushroom with the bread crumb stuffing.
6. Place the mushrooms in the greased air fryer basket in a single layer.
7. Set the temperature to 360°F. Set the timer and bake for 10 minutes.
8. Using tongs, remove the mushrooms from the air fryer, place them on a platter, and serve.

INGREDIENT TIP: Purchasing fresh mushrooms is hard because mushrooms in the supermarket are often covered with plastic wrap. Examine the mushrooms before you purchase them: You are looking for mushrooms free of slime, mold, or wrinkles, all of which mean they're older. Look for firm mushrooms instead. Before you prepare any mushroom dish, always wipe the mushrooms with a damp cloth, which will help get rid of any dirt and grit.

Per Serving: Calories: 216; Fat: 18g; Saturated fat: 3g; Carbohydrate: 12g; Fiber: 1g; Sugar: 2g; Protein: 4g; Iron: 2mg; Sodium: 683mg

AIR FRYER BACON-WRAPPED JALAPEÑO POPPERS

FAMILY FAVORITE, GLUTEN-FREE

This is a satisfying and easy appetizer. It has the great spicy flavor of the jalapeño pepper and the richness of cheese, all wrapped up in delicious bacon. A true family favorite, poppers are great for any occasion.

BAKE / 320°F

PREP TIME: 5 MINUTES

COOK TIME: 12 MINUTES

SERVES 12

12 jalapeño peppers

1 (8-ounce) package cream cheese, at room temperature

1 cup shredded Cheddar cheese

1 teaspoon onion powder

1 teaspoon salt

½ teaspoon freshly ground black pepper

12 slices bacon, cut in half

1. Spray the air fryer basket with olive oil.
2. Cut each pepper in half, then use a spoon to scrape out the veins and seeds.
3. In a small mixing bowl, mix together the cream cheese, Cheddar cheese, onion powder, salt, and pepper.
4. Using a small spoon, fill each pepper half with the cheese mixture.
5. Wrap each stuffed pepper half with a half slice of bacon.
6. Place the bacon-wrapped peppers into the greased air fryer basket in a single layer. (You may have to cook the peppers in more than one batch.)
7. Set the temperature for 320°F. Set the timer and bake for 12 minutes.
8. Using tongs, remove the peppers from the air fryer, place them on a platter, and serve.

INGREDIENT TIP: Be careful when you are seeding these peppers. The spicy part is not the pepper itself but the seeds. The seeds are extremely spicy and their oils can transfer to anything your hands come in contact with, so be sure to wash your hands thoroughly after seeding.

Per Serving: Calories: 212; Fat: 18g; Saturated fat: 9g; Carbohydrate: 2g; Fiber: 0g; Sugar: 1g; Protein: 11g; Iron: 1mg; Sodium: 747mg

SEAFOOD

< Lemon, Garlic, and Herb Salmon,
  page 60

AIR FRYER CAJUN SHRIMP

FAST, GLUTEN-FREE

Using a few basic spices from your pantry, you can whip up this smoky and spicy Cajun shrimp in no time. Serve this for lunch or dinner, as an appetizer or as finger food at a party. No matter what the occasion, this dish is a winner.

STEAM / 390°F

PREP TIME: 5 MINUTES

COOK TIME: 6 MINUTES

SERVES 2

12 ounces uncooked medium shrimp, peeled and deveined

1 teaspoon cayenne pepper

1 teaspoon Old Bay seasoning

½ teaspoon smoked paprika

2 tablespoons olive oil

1 teaspoon salt

1. Preheat the air fryer to 390°F.

2. Meanwhile, in a medium mixing bowl, combine the shrimp, cayenne pepper, Old Bay, paprika, olive oil, and salt. Toss the shrimp in the oil and spices until the shrimp is thoroughly coated with both.

3. Place the shrimp in the air fryer basket. Set the timer and steam for 3 minutes.

4. Remove the drawer and shake, so the shrimp redistribute in the basket for even cooking.

5. Reset the timer and steam for another 3 minutes.

6. Check that the shrimp are done. When they are cooked through, the flesh will be opaque. Add additional time if needed.

7. Plate, serve, and enjoy!

VARIATION TIP: For a complete meal, add 1 sliced onion, 1 sliced bell pepper, 1 (15.25-ounce) can sweet corn kernels, and double the amount of the seasonings and oil in step 2. Proceed with the recipe as instructed.

Per Serving: Calories: 286; Fat: 16g; Saturated fat: 2g; Carbohydrate: 1g; Fiber: 0g; Sugar: 0g; Protein: 37g; Iron: 6mg; Sodium: 1868mg

HOMEMADE AIR FRIED CRAB CAKE SLIDERS

FAMILY FAVORITE, FAST

This is one of the easiest and tastiest meals I have made in my air fryer. After we get home from the kids' activities, this recipe makes for a quick and healthy dinner when everyone is so famished that we can't wait another minute to eat. These sliders are also great to make ahead. Simply reheat when you're ready to eat.

FRY / 400°F

PREP TIME: 5 MINUTES

COOK TIME: 10 MINUTES

SERVES 4

1 pound crabmeat, shredded

¼ cup bread crumbs

2 teaspoons dried parsley

1 teaspoon salt

½ teaspoon freshly ground black pepper

1 large egg

2 tablespoons mayonnaise

1 teaspoon dry mustard

4 slider buns

Sliced tomato, lettuce leaves, and rémoulade sauce, for topping

1. Spray the air fryer basket with olive oil or spray an air fryer–size baking sheet with olive oil or cooking spray.

2. In a medium mixing bowl, combine the crabmeat, bread crumbs, parsley, salt, pepper, egg, mayonnaise, and dry mustard. Mix well.

3. Form the crab mixture into 4 equal patties. (If your patties are too wet, add an additional 1 to 2 tablespoons of bread crumbs.)

4. Place the crab cakes directly into the greased air fryer basket, or on the greased baking sheet set into the air fryer basket.

5. Set the temperature to 400°F. Set the timer and fry for 5 minutes.

6. Flip the crab cakes. Reset the timer and fry the crab cakes for 5 minutes more.

7. Serve on slider buns with sliced tomato, lettuce, and rémoulade sauce.

SUBSTITUTION TIP: Serve with a homemade aioli sauce instead of store-bought rémoulade. In a small bowl, combine ½ cup of mayonnaise, 2 tablespoons of lemon juice, 2 teaspoons of minced garlic, and ½ teaspoon of smoked paprika. Season with salt and pepper.

Per Serving: Calories: 294; Fat: 11g; Saturated fat: 2g; Carbohydrate: 20g; Fiber: 1g; Sugar: 3g; Protein: 27g; Iron: 2mg; Sodium: 1766mg

AIR FRIED LOBSTER TAILS

FAST, GLUTEN-FREE

Look for frozen lobster tails in the freezer case in the seafood department. The hardest part of this recipe is butterflying the lobster, but this allows the air fryer to steam the meat in the butter, making it extremely tender and rich.

STEAM / 380°F

PREP TIME: 5 MINUTES

COOK TIME: 8 MINUTES

SERVES 2

---

2 tablespoons unsalted butter, melted

1 tablespoon minced garlic

1 teaspoon salt

1 tablespoon minced fresh chives

2 (4- to 6-ounce) frozen lobster tails

1. In a small mixing bowl, combine the butter, garlic, salt, and chives.

2. Butterfly the lobster tail: Starting at the meaty end of the tail, use kitchen shears to cut down the center of the top shell. Stop when you reach the fanned, wide part of the tail. Carefully spread apart the meat and the shell along the cut line, but keep the meat attached where it connects to the wide part of the tail. Use your hand to gently disconnect the meat from the bottom of the shell. Lift the meat up and out of the shell (keeping it attached at the wide end). Close the shell under the meat, so the meat rests on top of the shell.

3. Place the lobster in the air fryer basket and generously brush the butter mixture over the meat.

4. Set the temperature to 380°F. Set the timer and steam for 4 minutes.

5. Open the air fryer and rotate the lobster tails. Brush them with more of the butter mixture.

6. Reset the timer and steam for 4 minutes more. The lobster is done when the meat is opaque.

INGREDIENT TIP: If you're using fresh lobster, the times will differ. Cook the lobster tails for 3 minutes, then rotate and cook for another 3 minutes. If your air fryer has a broil function, you can broil fresh or thawed lobster tails for about 6 minutes.

Per Serving: Calories: 255; Fat: 13g; Saturated fat: 7g; Carbohydrate: 2g; Fiber: 0g; Sugar: 0g; Protein: 32g; Iron: 0mg; Sodium: 1453mg

BACON-WRAPPED SCALLOPS

FAMILY FAVORITE, FAST, GLUTEN-FREE

This dish looks elegant on a platter but takes only about 5 minutes to assemble and 10 minutes to cook. Delight your guests or your family, and make this showstopper for dinner. They are also amazing as appetizers.

FRY / 370°F

PREP TIME: 5 MINUTES

COOK TIME: 10 MINUTES

SERVES 4

---

16 sea scallops

8 slices bacon, cut in half

8 toothpicks

Salt

Freshly ground black pepper

1. Using a paper towel, pat dry the scallops.
2. Wrap each scallop with a half slice of bacon. Secure the bacon with a toothpick.
3. Place the scallops into the air fryer in a single layer. (You may need to cook your scallops in more than one batch.)
4. Spray the scallops with olive oil, and season them with salt and pepper.
5. Set the temperature to 370°F. Set the timer and fry for 5 minutes.
6. Flip the scallops.
7. Reset your timer and cook the scallops for 5 minutes more.
8. Using tongs, remove the scallops from the air fryer basket. Plate, serve, and enjoy!

AIR FRYER TIP: Toothpicks become a kitchen staple when you start working with your air fryer. They help keep your food together while it's cooking. Otherwise, because of your air fryer's powerful fan, some foods can blow around the air fryer, which can be dangerous if they whip up into the fan directly.

Per Serving: Calories: 311; Fat: 17g; Saturated fat: 5g; Carbohydrate: 3g; Fiber: 0g; Sugar: 0g; Protein: 34g; Iron: 1mg; Sodium: 1110mg

LEMON PEPPER, BUTTER, AND CAJUN COD

GLUTEN-FREE

On nights when you're looking for something light and delicious, this dish will become your new go-to. It works with many different kinds of fish, including haddock, catfish, and other white fish.

BAKE / 360°F

PREP TIME: 5 MINUTES

COOK TIME: 12 MINUTES

SERVES 2

---

2 (8-ounce) cod fillets, cut to fit into the air fryer basket

1 tablespoon Cajun seasoning

½ teaspoon lemon pepper

1 teaspoon salt

½ teaspoon freshly ground black pepper

2 tablespoons unsalted butter, melted

1 lemon, cut into 4 wedges

1. Spray the air fryer basket with olive oil.

2. Place the fillets on a plate.

3. In a small mixing bowl, combine the Cajun seasoning, lemon pepper, salt, and pepper.

4. Rub the seasoning mix onto the fish.

5. Place the cod into the greased air fryer basket. Brush the top of each fillet with melted butter.

6. Set the temperature to 360°F. Set the timer and bake for 6 minutes.

7. After 6 minutes, open up your air fryer drawer and flip the fish. Brush the top of each fillet with more melted butter.

8. Reset the timer and bake for 6 minutes more.

9. Squeeze fresh lemon juice over the fillets.

SUBSTITUTION TIP: In this recipe, I used fresh cod, but you can easily swap it out for frozen cod. You will need to cook frozen cod for a total of 15 to 17 minutes. Remember to flip it halfway through cooking.

Per Serving: Calories: 283; Fat: 14g; Saturated fat: 7g; Carbohydrate: 0g; Fiber: 0g; Sugar: 0g; Protein: 40g; Iron: 0mg; Sodium: 1460mg .

SALMON PATTIES

FAMILY FAVORITE, FAST

If you keep your pantry stocked with a can or two of wild salmon, you can always make this delicious meal for a quick and easy lunch or dinner. These salmon patties are tender on the inside and flaky and golden brown on the outside. For something different and equally delicious, try this with canned tuna instead.

GRILL / 370°F

PREP TIME: 5 MINUTES

COOK TIME: 10 MINUTES

SERVES 4

---

1 (14.75-ounce) can wild salmon, drained

1 large egg

¼ cup diced onion

½ cup bread crumbs

1 teaspoon dried dill

½ teaspoon freshly ground black pepper

1 teaspoon salt

1 teaspoon Old Bay seasoning

1. Spray the air fryer basket with olive oil.
2. Put the salmon in a medium bowl and remove any bones or skin.
3. Add the egg, onion, bread crumbs, dill, pepper, salt, and Old Bay seasoning and mix well.
4. Form the salmon mixture into 4 equal patties.
5. Place the patties in the greased air fryer basket.
6. Set the temperature to 370°F. Set the timer and grill for 5 minutes.
7. Flip the patties. Reset the timer and grill the patties for 5 minutes more.
8. Plate, serve, and enjoy!

INGREDIENT TIP: Canned salmon contains bones and skin. I like to remove them, but they are edible and some people prefer to keep them since they are a source of nutrition, particularly calcium in the bones. If you prefer to keep them in, it's perfectly acceptable.

Per Serving: Calories: 239; Fat: 9g; Saturated fat: 2g; Carbohydrate: 11g; Fiber: 1g; Sugar: 1g; Protein: 27g; Iron: 2mg; Sodium: 901mg

LEMON, GARLIC, AND HERB SALMON

FAMILY FAVORITE, FAST, GLUTEN-FREE

There is nothing like a great piece of cooked salmon. With this recipe, the lemon, garlic, and herb sauce brings out the natural taste of the salmon. By using your air fryer, you will get salmon cooked to perfection. The whole family will love it.

BAKE / 400°F

PREP TIME: 5 MINUTES

COOK TIME: 10 MINUTES

SERVES 4

———

3 tablespoons unsalted butter

1 garlic clove, minced, or
½ teaspoon garlic powder

1 teaspoon salt

2 tablespoons freshly squeezed
lemon juice

1 tablespoon minced fresh parsley

1 teaspoon minced fresh dill

1 teaspoon salt

½ teaspoon freshly ground
black pepper

4 (4-ounce) salmon fillets

1. Line the air fryer basket with parchment paper.

2. In a small microwave-safe mixing bowl, combine the butter, garlic, salt, lemon juice, parsley, dill, salt, and pepper.

3. Place the bowl in the microwave and cook on low until the butter is completely melted, about 45 seconds.

4. Meanwhile, place the salmon fillets in the parchment-lined air fryer basket.

5. Spoon the sauce over the salmon.

6. Set the temperature to 400°F. Set the timer and bake for 10 minutes. Since you don't want to overcook the salmon, begin checking for doneness at about 8 minutes. Salmon is done when the flesh is opaque and flakes easily when tested with a fork.

———

AIR FRYER TIP: You can buy parchment paper made to fit many models of air fryers. Often, air fryer parchment is perforated, as well. Use air fryer parchment sheets to line the bottom of your air fryer basket. It's food-safe and you can place what you're cooking right on top of. Once your food is done cooking and the air fryer cools down, you simply pick up the parchment paper and throw it away.

———

Per Serving: Calories: 346; Fat: 22g; Saturated fat: 8g; Carbohydrate: 1g; Fiber: 0g; Sugar: 0g; Protein: 32g; Iron: 1mg; Sodium: 1300mg

POULTRY

< Air Fryer Grilled Chicken Fajitas,
  page 66

BUFFALO CHICKEN WINGS

FAMILY FAVORITE

Chicken wings were made for the air fryer, so they're the perfect food to start your air frying with. These are amazing. The chicken skin is nice and crispy, and when served piping hot directly from your air fryer, you can taste the perfect flavor in every bite. Serve your wings with carrot and celery sticks and blue cheese dressing.

FRY / 370°F

PREP TIME: 10 MINUTES

COOK TIME: 24 MINUTES

SERVES 4

———

8 tablespoons (1 stick) unsalted butter, melted

½ cup hot sauce

2 tablespoons white vinegar

2 teaspoons Worcestershire sauce

1 teaspoon garlic powder

½ cup all-purpose flour

16 frozen chicken wings

1. Preheat the air fryer to 370°F.
2. In a small saucepan over low heat, combine the butter, hot sauce, vinegar, Worcestershire sauce, and garlic. Mix well and bring to a simmer.
3. Pour the flour into a medium mixing bowl. Dredge the chicken wings in the flour.
4. Place the flour-coated wings into the air fryer basket.
5. Set the timer and fry for 12 minutes.
6. Using tongs, flip the wings.
7. Reset the timer and fry for 12 minutes more.
8. Release the air fryer basket from the drawer. Turn out the chicken wings into a large mixing bowl, then pour the sauce over them.
9. Serve and enjoy!

VARIATION TIP: Buffalo chicken wings are irresistible when they're served with a homemade blue cheese dressing. Mix together ½ cup of crumbled blue cheese, ½ cup of sour cream, ¼ cup of mayonnaise, 1 teaspoon of milk, 1 tablespoon of lemon juice, and a dash each of salt and pepper. Mix well, and chill for at least 1 hour before serving.

Per Serving: Calories: 705; Fat: 55g; Saturated fat: 23g; Carbohydrate: 14g; Fiber: 1g; Sugar: 1g; Protein: 38g; Iron: 3mg; Sodium: 1096mg

PARMESAN CHICKEN TENDERS

FAMILY FAVORITE, FAST

If you have small kids, this dish is indispensable. The chicken tenders are very lightly battered and have loads of flavor, thanks to the Parmesan cheese.

BAKE / 370°F

PREP TIME: 5 MINUTES

COOK TIME: 8 MINUTES

SERVES 4

---

1 pound chicken tenderloins

3 large egg whites

½ cup Italian-style bread crumbs

¼ cup grated Parmesan cheese

1. Spray the air fryer basket with olive oil.
2. Trim off any white fat from the chicken tenders.
3. In a small bowl, beat the egg whites until frothy.
4. In a separate small mixing bowl, combine the bread crumbs and Parmesan cheese. Mix well.
5. Dip the chicken tenders into the egg mixture, then into the Parmesan and bread crumbs. Shake off any excess breading.
6. Place the chicken tenders in the greased air fryer basket in a single layer. (You may need to bake the chicken tenders in more than one batch.) Generously spray the chicken with olive oil to avoid powdery, uncooked breading.
7. Set the temperature to 370°F. Set the timer and bake for 4 minutes.
8. Using tongs, flip the chicken tenders and bake for 4 minutes more.
9. Check that the chicken has reached an internal temperature of 165°F. Add cooking time if needed.
10. Once the chicken is fully cooked, plate, serve, and enjoy!

VARIATION TIP: For a twist on this dish, add about 2 tablespoons of minced garlic to the bread crumb and Parmesan cheese mixture. It will add another level of flavor.

Per Serving: Calories: 210; Fat: 4g; Saturated fat: 1g; Carbohydrate: 10g; Fiber: 1g; Sugar: 1g; Protein: 33g; Iron: 1mg; Sodium: 390mg

AIR FRYER GRILLED CHICKEN FAJITAS

FAMILY FAVORITE, GLUTEN-FREE

Now you can make authentic chickens at home. Maybe host a make-your-own fajita gathering at your house and show off your air fryer skills. Serve with soft tortillas, if you like.

GRILL / 350°F

PREP TIME: 10 MINUTES

COOK TIME: 14 MINUTES

SERVES 4

---

1 pound chicken tenders

1 onion, sliced

1 yellow bell pepper, diced

1 red bell pepper, diced

1 orange bell pepper, diced

2 tablespoons olive oil

1 tablespoon fajita seasoning mix

1. Slice the chicken into thin strips.
2. In a large mixing bowl, combine the chicken, onion, and peppers.
3. Add the olive oil and fajita seasoning and mix well, so that the chicken and vegetables are thoroughly covered with oil.
4. Place the chicken and vegetable mixture into the air fryer basket in a single layer.
5. Set the temperature to 350°F. Set the timer and grill for 7 minutes.
6. Shake the basket and use tongs to flip the chicken.
7. Reset the timer and grill for 7 minutes more, or until the chicken is cooked through and the juices run clear.
8. Once the chicken is fully cooked, transfer it to a platter and serve.

SUBSTITUTION TIP: This is one of my family's favorite meals, which I change up by substituting flank steak or shrimp for the chicken. Either will cook in about the same amount of time as the chicken.

Per Serving: Calories: 222; Fat: 9g; Saturated fat: 1g; Carbohydrate: 10g; Fiber: 2g; Sugar: 3g; Protein: 27g; Iron: 1mg; Sodium: 135mg

EASY LEMON CHICKEN THIGHS

FAMILY FAVORITE, GLUTEN-FREE

Serve these flavorful chicken thighs with rice and a side of vegetables and you'll have a healthy and delicious meal on your table in about 25 minutes.

BAKE / 350°F

PREP TIME: 5 MINUTES

COOK TIME: 20 MINUTES

SERVES 4

———————

4 to 6 chicken thighs

1 teaspoon salt

1 teaspoon freshly ground black pepper

2 tablespoons olive oil

2 tablespoons Italian seasoning

2 tablespoons freshly squeezed lemon juice

1 lemon, sliced

1. Place the chicken thighs in a medium mixing bowl and season them with the salt and pepper.
2. Add the olive oil, Italian seasoning, and lemon juice and toss until the chicken thighs are thoroughly coated with oil.
3. Add the sliced lemons.
4. Place the chicken thighs into the air fryer basket in a single layer.
5. Set the temperature to 350°F. Set the timer and cook for 10 minutes.
6. Using tongs, flip the chicken.
7. Reset the timer and cook for 10 minutes more.
8. Check that the chicken has reached an internal temperature of 165°F. Add cooking time if needed.
9. Once the chicken is fully cooked, plate, serve, and enjoy!

VARIATION TIP: There is so much you can do with this dish. I sometimes add 2 tablespoons of chopped garlic to make a delicious lemon and garlic dish. You can also incorporate fresh herbs: Add about 2 tablespoons of fresh thyme, rosemary, or oregano—or all three—to vary the flavors and aromas.

Per Serving: Calories: 325; Fat: 26g; Saturated fat: 6g; Carbohydrate: 1g; Fiber: 0g; Sugar: 1g; Protein: 20g; Iron: 1mg; Sodium: 670mg

AIR FRYER SOUTHERN FRIED CHICKEN

Everyone loves fried chicken. There are countless restaurants in America that specialize in selling fried chicken. Fried used to be synonymous with deep-frying, but now, with the air fryer, you can trade the cups of oil needed for deep-frying with just a few spritzes while still producing the signature crispy skin and juicy meat that make this classic so beloved.

FRY / 390°F

PREP TIME: 15 MINUTES, PLUS 1 HOUR TO MARINATE

COOK TIME: 26 MINUTES

SERVES 4

½ cup buttermilk

2 teaspoons salt, plus 1 tablespoon

1 teaspoon freshly ground black pepper

1 pound chicken thighs and drumsticks

1 cup all-purpose flour

2 teaspoons onion powder

2 teaspoons garlic powder

½ teaspoon sweet paprika

1. In a large mixing bowl, whisk together the buttermilk, 2 teaspoons of salt, and pepper.

2. Add the chicken pieces to the bowl, and let the chicken marinate for at least an hour, covered, in the refrigerator.

3. About 5 minutes before the chicken is done marinating, prepare the dredging mixture. In a large mixing bowl, combine the flour, 1 tablespoon of salt, onion powder, garlic powder, and paprika.

4. Spray the air fryer basket with olive oil.

5. Remove the chicken from the buttermilk mixture and dredge it in the flour mixture. Shake off any excess flour.

6. Place the chicken pieces into the greased air fryer basket in a single layer, leaving space between each piece. (You may have to fry the chicken in more than one batch.) Spray the chicken generously with olive oil.

7. Set the temperature to 390°F. Set the timer and cook for 13 minutes.

8. Using tongs, flip the chicken. Spray generously with olive oil.

9. Reset the timer and fry for 13 minutes more.

10. Check that the chicken has reached an internal temperature of 165°F. Add cooking time if needed.

11. Once the chicken is fully cooked, plate, serve, and enjoy!

AIR FRYER TIP: This is one of the recipes where overcrowding your chicken will produce uneven results. If the pieces are too close, the batter will stick, causing it to rub off.

Per Serving: Calories: 377; Fat: 18g; Saturated fat: 5g; Carbohydrate: 28g; Fiber: 1g; Sugar: 2g; Protein: 25g; Iron: 3mg; Sodium: 1182mg

AIR FRYER GRILLED CHICKEN BREASTS

FAMILY FAVORITE, GLUTEN-FREE

This is a foolproof recipe for making a tender grilled chicken breast in the air fryer. You can use it in any recipe that calls for cooked chicken, such as pot pie or even a simple chicken salad. This is a winner for any meal and my kids love it!

GRILL / 370°F

PREP TIME: 5 MINUTES

COOK TIME: 14 MINUTES

SERVES 4

½ teaspoon garlic powder

1 teaspoon salt

½ teaspoon freshly ground black pepper

1 teaspoon dried parsley

2 tablespoons olive oil, divided

4 boneless, skinless chicken breasts

1. In a small mixing bowl, mix together the garlic powder, salt, pepper, and parsley.
2. Using 1 tablespoon of olive oil and half of the seasoning mix, rub each chicken breast with oil and seasonings.
3. Place the chicken breast in the air fryer basket.
4. Set the temperature to 370°F. Set the timer and grill for 7 minutes.
5. Using tongs, flip the chicken and brush the remaining olive oil and spices onto the chicken.
6. Reset the timer and grill for 7 minutes more.
7. Check that the chicken has reached an internal temperature of 165°F. Add cooking time if needed.
8. Once the chicken is fully cooked, transfer it to a platter and serve.

VARIATION TIP: This is a great base recipe for a number of other dishes, such as broccoli stuffed chicken. After step 2, simply make a pocket with a knife in the center of the chicken breast. To make enough for the 4 chicken breasts above, cook (per package instructions) a 10-ounce bag of frozen broccoli and mix it with ½ cup of shredded Cheddar cheese. Stuff the broccoli and cheese mixture into the pocket and proceed with the recipe as instructed.

Per Serving: Calories: 182; Fat: 9g; Saturated fat: 1g; Carbohydrate: 0g; Fiber: 0g; Sugar: 0g; Protein: 26g; Iron: 1mg; Sodium: 657mg

CRISPY AIR FRYER BUTTER CHICKEN

This is a classic dish, using a simple package cf Ritz crackers. The result is a juicy and delicious meal. I usually serve this beside a plate of steaming hot Fresh Homemade Potato Wedges (page 47), with a simple side salad.

BAKE / 370°F

PREP TIME: 5 MINUTES

COOK TIME: 14 MINUTES

SERVES 2

---

2 (8-ounce) boneless, skinless chicken breasts

1 sleeve Ritz crackers

4 tablespoons (½ stick) cold unsalted butter, cut into 1-tablespoon slices

1. Spray the air fryer basket with olive oil, or spray an air fryer–size baking sheet with olive oil or cooking spray.

2. Dip the chicken breasts in water.

3. Put the crackers in a resealable plastic bag. Using a mallet or your hands, crush the crackers.

4. Place the chicken breasts inside the bag one at a time and coat them with the cracker crumbs.

5. Place the chicken in the greased air fryer basket, or on the greased baking sheet set into the air fryer basket.

6. Put 1 to 2 dabs of butter onto each piece of chicken.

7. Set the temperature to 370°F. Set the timer and bake for 7 minutes.

8. Using tongs, flip the chicken. Spray the chicken generously with olive oil to avoid uncooked breading.

9. Reset the timer and bake for 7 minutes more.

10. Check that the chicken has reached an internal temperature of 165°F. Add cooking time if needed.

11. Using tongs, remove the chicken from the air fryer and serve.

SUBSTITUTION TIP: To add a twist with ranch seasoning, instead of using crackers in steps 3 and 4, put ½ cup of mayonnaise into a small bowl, then in another bowl combine 1 package of ranch dressing mix and 1 cup of bread crumbs. Dip each chicken breast in the mayonnaise to thinly coat, then in the ranch breading, and then place the chicken in the greased air fryer basket. Spray generously with olive oil and proceed with steps 7 through 11 as directed.

Per Serving: Calories: 750; Fat: 40g; Saturated fat: 18g; Carbohydrate: 38g; Fiber: 2g; Sugar: 5g; Protein: 57g; Iron: 4mg; Sodium: 853mg

LIGHT AND AIRY BREADED CHICKEN BREASTS

By using just a few ingredients—most of them already in your pantry—you can make this quick and delicious chicken dish. It also makes amazing leftovers. Serve with an easy garden salad for a healthy, satisfying meal.

FRY / 370°F

PREP TIME: 5 MINUTES

COOK TIME: 14 MINUTES

SERVES 2

---

2 large eggs

1 cup bread crumbs or panko bread crumbs

1 teaspoon Italian seasoning

4 to 5 tablespoons vegetable oil

2 (8-ounce) boneless, skinless chicken breasts

1. Preheat the air fryer to 370°F. Spray the air fryer basket (or an air fryer–size baking sheet) with olive oil or cooking spray.
2. In a small mixing bowl, beat the eggs until frothy.
3. In a separate small mixing bowl, mix together the bread crumbs, Italian seasoning, and oil.
4. Dip the chicken in the egg mixture, then in the bread crumb mixture.
5. Place the chicken directly into the greased air fryer basket, or on the greased baking sheet set into the basket.
6. Spray the chicken generously and thoroughly with olive oil to avoid powdery, uncooked breading.
7. Set the timer and fry for 7 minutes.
8. Using tongs, flip the chicken and generously spray it with olive oil.
9. Reset the timer and fry for 7 minutes more.
10. Check that the chicken has reached an internal temperature of 165°F. Add cooking time if needed.
11. Once the chicken is fully cooked, use tongs to remove it from the air fryer and serve.

VARIATION TIP: Mix it up by adding 1 tablespoon of minced garlic and ⅔ cup of grated Parmesan cheese to the bread crumb mixture.

Per Serving: Calories: 833; Fat: 46g; Saturated fat: 5g; Carbohydrate: 40g; Fiber: 2g; Sugar: 4g; Protein: 65g; Iron: 5mg; Sodium: 609mg

AIR FRYER CHICKEN PARMESAN

FAMILY FAVORITE

A twist on the classic Italian dish, this recipe avoids the heavy amounts of oil and gets to the heart of the matter: a lightly battered piece of chicken, a great sauce, and a topping of melted cheese. This is comfort food at its best.

BAKE / 360°F

PREP TIME: 5 MINUTES

COOK TIME: 14 MINUTES

SERVES 4

2 (8-ounce) boneless, skinless chicken breasts

2 large eggs

1 cup Italian-style bread crumbs

¼ cup shredded Parmesan cheese

½ cup marinara sauce

½ cup shredded mozzarella cheese

1. Preheat the air fryer to 360°F. Spray an air fryer–size baking sheet with olive oil or cooking spray.

2. Using a mallet or rolling pin, flatten the chicken breasts to about ¼ inch thick.

3. In a small mixing bowl, beat the eggs until frothy. In another small mixing bowl, mix together the bread crumbs and Parmesan cheese.

4. Dip the chicken in the egg, then in the bread crumb mixture.

5. Place the chicken on the greased baking sheet. Set the baking sheet into the air fryer basket.

6. Spray the chicken generously with olive oil to avoid powdery, uncooked breading.

7. Set the timer and bake for 7 minutes, or until cooked through and the juices run clear.

8. Flip the chicken and pour the marinara sauce over the chicken. Sprinkle with the mozzarella cheese. Reset the timer and bake for another 7 minutes.

9. Once the chicken Parmesan is fully cooked, use tongs to remove it from the air fryer and serve.

COOKING TIP: Make a double batch and use the leftovers to make a chicken Parmesan sandwich. I like to reheat the chicken with some additional marinara sauce and serve it on a hamburger bun.

Per Serving: Calories: 331; Fat: 9g; Saturated fat: 4g; Carbohydrate: 23g; Fiber: 2g; Sugar: 4g; Protein: 39g; Iron: 3mg; Sodium: 876mg

AIR FRYER CHICKEN DRUMSTICKS WITH A SWEET RUB

FAMILY FAVORITE, GLUTEN-FREE

Nothing is as fun to eat as chicken drumsticks. They are great at any time of day. Hot or cold, at the kitchen table or on a picnic, this classic finger food brings out the kid in everyone. The sweet rub in this version enhances the rich, savory flavor of the dark meat.

BAKE / 390°F

PREP TIME: 5 MINUTES

COOK TIME: 20 MINUTES

SERVES 4

¼ cup brown sugar

1 tablespoon salt

½ teaspoon freshly ground black pepper

1 teaspoon chili powder

1 teaspoon smoked paprika

1 teaspoon dry mustard

1 teaspoon garlic powder

1 teaspoon onion powder

4 to 6 chicken drumsticks

2 tablespoons olive oil

1. In a small mixing bowl, combine the brown sugar, salt, pepper, chili powder, paprika, mustard, garlic powder, and onion powder.
2. Using a paper towel, wipe any moisture off the chicken.
3. Put the chicken drumsticks into a large resealable plastic bag, then pour in the dry rub. Seal the bag.
4. Shake the bag to coat the chicken.
5. Place the drumsticks in the air fryer basket. Brush the drumsticks with olive oil.
6. Set the temperature to 390°F. Set the timer and bake for 10 minutes.
7. Using tongs, flip the drumsticks, and brush them with olive oil.
8. Reset the timer and bake for 10 minutes more.
9. Check that the chicken has reached an internal temperature of 165°F. Add cooking time if needed.
10. Once the chicken is fully cooked, transfer it to a platter and serve.

SUBSTITUTION TIP: Turkey drumsticks also work for this recipe. Increase the total cooking time to 30 minutes.

Per Serving: Calories: 317; Fat: 22g; Saturated fat: 5g; Carbohydrate: 11g; Fiber: 1g; Sugar: 9g; Protein: 22g; Iron: 2mg; Sodium: 1844mg

AIR FRYER CORNISH HEN

GLUTEN-FREE

There is nothing like making a Cornish hen in your air fryer. It makes a wonderful fall meal. Make it special by serving it with traditional Thanksgiving side dishes, including mashed potatoes and gravy, for a great Sunday dinner. The skin becomes really nice and juicy with a great crunch to it.

ROAST / 390°F

PREP TIME: 5 MINUTES

COOK TIME: 30 MINUTES

SERVES 2

---

2 tablespoons Montreal chicken seasoning

1 (1½- to 2-pound) Cornish hen

1. Preheat the air fryer to 390°F.

2. Rub the seasoning over the chicken, coating it thoroughly.

3. Place the chicken in the air fryer basket. Set the timer and roast for 15 minutes.

4. Flip the chicken and cook for another 15 minutes.

5. Check that the chicken has reached an internal temperature of 165°F. Add cooking time if needed.

VARIATION TIP: A Cornish hen is especially nice when it's well seasoned. To make your own chicken rub, combine the following ingredients in a small bowl: ¼ cup of brown sugar, ¼ cup of paprika, ¼ cup of coarse salt, 2 tablespoons of black pepper, 2 tablespoons of garlic powder, 2 tablespoons of onion powder, and a pinch of cayenne pepper. This will make enough for about five Cornish hens; I usually keep some on hand. It's an excellent rub for any chicken or pork dish.

Per Serving: Calories: 520; Fat: 36g; Saturated fat: 10g; Carbohydrate: 0g; Fiber: 0g; Sugar: 0g; Protein: 45g; Iron: 2mg; Sodium: 758mg

AIR FRIED TURKEY WINGS

FAMILY FAVORITE, GLUTEN-FREE

Turkey is not just for the holidays. This is an easy way to serve turkey year-round. There is nothing like biting into a delicious and flavorful turkey wing. They are a treat for the entire family—and they are so much meatier than chicken wings.

ROAST / 380°F

PREP TIME: 5 MINUTES

COOK TIME: 26 MINUTES

SERVES 4

———

2 pounds turkey wings

3 tablespoons olive oil or sesame oil

3 to 4 tablespoons chicken rub
(any type; see page 75)

1. Put the turkey wings in a large mixing bowl.

2. Pour the olive oil into the bowl and add the rub.

3. Using your hands, rub the oil mixture over the turkey wings.

4. Place the turkey wings in the air fryer basket.

5. Set the temperature to 380°F. Set the timer and roast for 13 minutes.

6. Using tongs, flip the wings.

7. Reset the timer and roast for 13 minutes more.

8. Remove the turkey wings from the air fryer, plate, and serve.

VARIATION TIP: You can convert any chicken wing recipe to a turkey wing recipe. You might need to increase the amount of sauce, but use this recipe as a guide for cooking time and temperature.

Per Serving: Calories: 521; Fat: 34g; Saturated fat: 2g; Carbohydrate: 4g; Fiber: 0g; Sugar: 0g; Protein: 52g; Iron: 0mg; Sodium: 600mg

AIR FRIED TURKEY BREAST

FAMILY FAVORITE, GLUTEN-FREE

The air fryer creates the most delicious roast turkey. The meat is moist and savory, while the skin is light and crispy. This would be a welcome Sunday dinner in any household.

ROAST / 350°F

PREP TIME: 5 MINUTES

COOK TIME: 45 TO 55 MINUTES

SERVES 4

———

2 tablespoons unsalted butter

1 teaspoon salt

½ teaspoon freshly ground black pepper

1 teaspoon dried thyme

1 teaspoon dried oregano

1 (3½-pound) boneless turkey breast

1 tablespoon olive oil

1. Melt the butter in a small microwave-safe bowl on low for about 45 seconds.
2. Add the salt, pepper, thyme, and oregano to the melted butter. Let the butter cool until you can handle it without burning yourself.
3. Rub the butter mixture all over the turkey breast, then rub on the olive oil, over the butter.
4. Place the turkey breast in the air fryer basket, skin-side down.
5. Set the temperature to 350°F. Set the timer and roast for 20 minutes.
6. Using tongs, flip the turkey.
7. Reset the timer and roast the turkey breast for another 30 minutes. Check that it has reached an internal temperature of 165°F. Add cooking time if needed.
8. Using tongs, remove the turkey from the air fryer and let rest for about 10 minutes before carving.

SUBSTITUTION TIP: You can make a great barbecue turkey rub from items in your pantry. In a small bowl, use a fork to combine 1 stick of softened unsalted butter, 5 tablespoons of brown sugar, 2 tablespoons of paprika, 1 tablespoon of onion powder, 2 teaspoons of salt, and 2 teaspoons of chili powder. Rub this mixture underneath the turkey skin instead of using the melted butter rub. Next, rub the olive oil all over the turkey breast, and proceed with steps 4 through 8.

Per Serving: Calories: 484; Fat: 11g; Saturated fat: 4g; Carbohydrate: 1g; Fiber: 0g; Sugar: 0g; Protein: 95g; Iron: 1mg; Sodium: 623mg

BEEF, PORK, AND LAMB

< Air Fryer Hamburgers,
  page 85

AIR FRYER STEAK TIPS

Steak tips were made for the air fryer. They are naturally cut into the same size pieces, and cooking them at high heat really brings out the flavor of the steak and the marinade. They will come out tender and delicious every time.

FRY / 400°F

PREP TIME: 5 MINUTES, PLUS 1 HOUR TO MARINATE

COOK TIME: 8 MINUTES

SERVES 4

———

⅓ cup soy sauce

1 cup water

¼ cup freshly squeezed lemon juice

3 tablespoons brown sugar

1 teaspoon garlic powder

1 teaspoon ground ginger

1 teaspoon dried parsley

2 pounds steak tips, cut into 1-inch cubes

1. In a large mixing bowl, make the marinade. Mix together the soy sauce, water, lemon juice, brown sugar, garlic powder, ginger, and parsley.

2. Place the meat in the marinade, then cover and refrigerate for at least 1 hour.

3. Preheat the air fryer to 400°F. Spray the air fryer basket with olive oil.

4. When the steak is done marinating, place it in the greased air fryer basket.

5. Set the timer and cook for 4 minutes.

6. Using tongs, flip the meat.

7. Reset the timer and cook for 4 minutes more.

SUBSTITUTION TIP: Changing out the marinade will result in a different steak tip dinner every night. One of my family's other favorite marinades requires only three ingredients: 1 cup of Italian dressing, 2 tablespoons of steak sauce, and 1 tablespoon of Worcestershire sauce.

Per Serving: Calories: 347; Fat: 9g; Saturated fat: 1g; Carbohydrate: 9g; Fiber: 0g; Sugar: 7g; Protein: 53g; Iron: 1mg; Sodium: 1203mg

AIR FRIED BEEF STIR-FRY

FAMILY FAVORITE

The beef strips in this dish get crisp on the outside while remaining tender on the inside. For an easy meal, serve this stir-fry with a side of rice.

STEAM / FRY / 200°F / 360°F

PREP TIME: 10 MINUTES, PLUS 30 MINUTES TO MARINATE

COOK TIME: 10 MINUTES

SERVES 4 TO 6

FOR THE MARINADE

¼ cup hoisin sauce

2 teaspoons minced garlic

1 teaspoon sesame oil

1 tablespoon soy sauce

1 teaspoon ground ginger

¼ cup water

FOR THE STIR-FRY

1 pound beef top sirloin steak, cut into 1-inch strips

½ cup diced red onion

1 green bell pepper, cut into 1-inch strips

1 red bell pepper, cut into 1-inch strips

1 yellow bell pepper, cut into 1-inch strips

1 pound of broccoli florets

1 teaspoon stir-fry oil

1. In a small mixing bowl, make the marinade. Mix together the hoisin sauce, garlic, sesame oil, soy sauce, ginger, and water.

2. Add the steak, then cover and let marinate in the refrigerator for about 30 minutes.

3. In a large bowl, combine the vegetables and the stir-fry oil and toss until the vegetables are thoroughly coated with oil.

4. Place the vegetables in the air fryer basket.

5. Set the temperature to 200°F. Set the timer and steam for 2 minutes. Check and make sure that the vegetables are soft. If not, add another 2 to 3 minutes.

6. Once the vegetables are soft, transfer them to a large bowl and place the meat into the air fryer.

7. Set the temperature to 360°F. Set the timer and fry for 4 minutes.

8. Check the meat to make sure it's fully cooked. If not, add another 2 minutes.

9. Pour the vegetables back into the air fryer basket and shake.

10. Release the air fryer basket. Pour the meat and vegetables into a bowl and serve.

INGREDIENT TIP: Stir-fry oil is usually found in the international aisle of the supermarket. It has its own distinctive flavor, as it often is infused with chiles. Some stir-fry oils are also flavored with garlic, ginger, onion, or other spices.

Per Serving: Calories: 284; Fat: 8g; Saturated fat: 1g; Carbohydrate: 24g; Fiber: 5g; Sugar: 9g; Protein: 31g; Iron: 2mg; Sodium: 525mg

AIR FRYER CARNE ASADA TACOS

FAMILY FAVORITE, GLUTEN-FREE

This is a common Mexican dish, also known as steak street tacos. Most commonly, the meat is served in a small (taco-size) soft tortilla—you can choose from flour, corn, or gluten-free varieties. But it is also great served in taco shells, in quesadillas, as a topping for nachos, or even on its own.

GRILL / 400°F

PREP TIME: 5 MINUTES

COOK TIME: 14 MINUTES

SERVES 4

1½ pounds flank steak

Salt

Freshly ground black pepper

⅓ cup olive oil

⅓ cup freshly squeezed lime juice

½ cup chopped fresh cilantro

4 teaspoons minced garlic

1 teaspoon ground cumin

1 teaspoon chili powder

1. Spray the air fryer basket with olive oil.
2. Place the flank steak in a large mixing bowl. Season with salt and pepper.
3. Add the olive oil, lime juice, cilantro, garlic, cumin, and chili powder and toss to coat the steak.
4. For the best flavor, let the steak marinate in the refrigerator for about 1 hour.
5. Place the steak in the air fryer basket.
6. Set the temperature to 400°F. Set the timer and grill for 7 minutes
7. Using tongs, flip the steak.
8. Reset the timer and grill for 7 minutes more.
9. Cook the steak to your desired level of doneness. For medium-rare, cook to an internal temperature of 135°F, or for medium, 145°F. Be careful not to overcook the steak, or it will dry out.
10. Let the steak rest for about 5 minutes, then cut into strips.

VARIATION TIP: Serve this up with homemade *pico de gallo*, which is really easy to make. Dice and mix together 1 red onion, 4 Roma tomatoes, ½ cup of fresh cilantro, and 1 jalapeño pepper (seeded). Add the juice of 1 lime and 1 teaspoon of salt. Mix well and serve on top of the tacos.

Per Serving: Calories: 371; Fat: 22g; Saturated fat: 1g; Carbohydrate: 4g; Fiber: 1g; Sugar: 1g; Protein: 38g; Iron: 1mg; Sodium: 67mg

AIR FRIED CHICKEN-FRIED STEAK

Chicken-fried steak is actually made from cube steaks. The method of preparing this dish is similar to how one would fry up chicken, hence the name. This dish is a Southern favorite, traditionally served with a rich gravy; sometimes the gravy has sausage and sometimes not.

FRY / 400°F

PREP TIME: 10 MINUTES

COOK TIME: 8 MINUTES

SERVES 4 TO 6

1½ cups all-purpose flour

1 teaspoon freshly ground black pepper

1 teaspoon salt

½ teaspoon smoked paprika

½ teaspoon onion powder

½ teaspoon garlic powder

½ teaspoon baking soda

½ teaspoon baking powder

1½ cup buttermilk

2 tablespoons hot sauce

2 large eggs

4 cube steaks

1. Spray the air fryer basket with olive oil.
2. In a small mixing bowl, mix together the flour, pepper, salt, paprika, onion powder, garlic powder, baking soda, and baking powder.
3. In a separate small mixing bowl, mix together the buttermilk, hot sauce, and eggs.
4. Dip the cube steaks in the flour mixture, shaking off any excess, then dip them in the buttermilk mixture, shaking off the excess, then dip them back in the flour mixture.
5. As you complete the cycle, place the steaks in the greased air fryer basket in a single layer. Be careful not to overcrowd the basket. Spray the coated steaks generously with olive oil.
6. Set the temperature to 400°F. Set the timer and fry for 4 minutes.
7. Using tongs, flip the steaks. Spray generously with olive oil.
8. Reset the timer and fry for 4 minutes more.

VARIATION TIP: A great and easy way to jazz up this meal is to serve it with homemade gravy. In a small saucepan, melt 4 tablespoons of butter, then mix in ¼ cup of flour, whisking until you have a nice golden-brown color. Next, whisk in 2 cups of milk and ½ cup of whipping cream; continue to whisk at a slow simmer for about 5 minutes. Season with salt and pepper.

Per Serving: Calories: 385; Fat: 8g; Saturated fat: 1g; Carbohydrate: 42g; Fiber: 2g; Sugar: 5g; Protein: 36g; Iron: 3mg; Sodium: 1060mg

AIR FRIED GRILLED RIB EYE WITH HERB BUTTER

FAMILY FAVORITE, GLUTEN-FREE

Who said you can't grill a steak in the air fryer? Served with a pat of herb butter, this steak is one of the tastiest you will ever have. It is a classic recipe and an all-around winner.

GRILL / 400°F

PREP TIME: 5 MINUTES, PLUS 1 HOUR TO CHILL

COOK TIME: 8 MINUTES

SERVES 4

FOR THE HERB BUTTER

1 cup (2 sticks) unsalted butter, at room temperature

1 garlic clove, roasted and peeled

1 tablespoon salt

1 teaspoon freshly ground black pepper

1 teaspoon minced shallot

1 teaspoon minced fresh parsley

1 teaspoon minced fresh sage

1 teaspoon minced fresh rosemary

FOR THE STEAK

4 (10- to 12-ounce) rib eye steaks

Salt

Freshly ground black pepper

TO MAKE THE HERB BUTTER

1. In a small mixing bowl, combine the butter, roasted garlic, salt, pepper, shallot, parsley, sage, and rosemary until the herbs are fully and evenly incorporated into the butter.

2. Cover the butter and refrigerate for about 1 hour.

TO MAKE THE STEAK

1. Preheat the air fryer to 400°F.

2. Season the steaks with salt and pepper.

3. Place the steaks into the air fryer basket. Grill for 4 minutes.

4. Using tongs, flip the steaks.

5. Reset the timer and grill for 4 minutes more. Cook the steaks to your desired level of doneness. For medium-rare, cook to an internal temperature of 135°F, or for medium, 145°F.

6. Place a dab of the butter on each steak. (Keep any remaining herb butter in the refrigerator for up to two days.)

COOKING TIP: One thing to remember when making steaks in the air fryer is that the thickness of the steak will determine your cooking time. The thicker the steak, the more you need to watch and rotate, or flip, the steak so that each side gets adequately cooked without getting charred.

Per Serving: Calories: 586; Fat: 36g; Saturated fat: 19g; Carbohydrate: 5g; Fiber: 0g; Sugar: 0g; Protein: 61g; Iron: 8mg; Sodium: 821mg

AIR FRYER HAMBURGERS

FAMILY FAVORITE, FAST

Nothing beats a classic American burger—except a classic American burger with bacon on top! This burger is absolutely juicy and delicious from air fryer to table. These are great for a party, where you can offer a variety of toppings and everyone can create their own signature burgers.

GRILL / 400°F

PREP TIME: 5 MINUTES

COOK TIME: 8 MINUTES

SERVES 4

———

2 slices crustless bread

¼ cup milk

1½ pounds lean ground beef

1 teaspoon salt

½ teaspoon freshly ground black pepper

1 teaspoon minced garlic

4 hamburger buns

6 slices Foolproof Air Fryer Bacon (page 30), for topping (optional)

Lettuce, sliced tomato, and pickle, for topping (optional)

1. Cut the bread into 1-inch pieces.
2. Put the bread pieces in a small mixing bowl and pour the milk over them. Let sit for about 5 minutes.
3. In a medium mixing bowl, add the ground beef, the bread and milk mixture, salt, pepper, and minced garlic.
4. Using your hands, mix well, making sure that the bread and milk mixture is broken down.
5. Divide the meat into fourths and form into patties. You should have 4 (6-ounce) patties.
6. Place the patties into the air fryer basket.
7. Set the temperature tor 400°F. Set the timer and grill for 4 minutes.
8. Using a spatula, flip and cook for 4 minutes more.
9. Assemble your hamburger by placing it in a hamburger bun and topping each burger with 1 or 2 slices of cooked bacon. Serve with a choice of toppings.

COOKING TIP: Another American classic you can make in the air fryer is hot dogs. To cook a hot dog, place it in the air fryer basket, air fry for 4 minutes at 400°F, then place the hot dog in a bun and air fry the hot dog inside the bun for another 2 minutes.

Per Serving: Calories: 558; Fat: 27g; Saturated fat: 9g; Carbohydrate: 29g; Fiber: 2g; Sugar: 4g; Protein: 50g; Iron: 6mg; Sodium: 1647mg

OLD-FASHIONED AIR FRYER MEATLOAF

FAMILY FAVORITE

This is one of America's favorite comfort foods. Kids love the simple ketchup topping, and you will like the savory flavor of the diced onions and sautéed green peppers, which bring out the flavor of the meat.

BAKE / 330°F

PREP TIME: 10 MINUTES

COOK TIME: 15 MINUTES

SERVES 4

2 tablespoons unsalted butter

½ cup diced onion

½ cup diced green bell pepper

1 pound lean ground beef

1 pound ground pork

2 large eggs

1 tablespoon Worcestershire sauce

1 tablespoon soy sauce

1 teaspoon salt

½ teaspoon freshly ground black pepper

1 cup bread crumbs, divided

⅓ cup ketchup, divided

1. Spray 3 mini loaf pans with cooking spray.
2. Heat the butter in a medium sauté pan or skillet over medium-low heat. Add the onions and green peppers and sauté until both are tender. Let the onions and green peppers cool to room temperature.
3. Meanwhile, in a large bowl, combine the beef and pork.
4. Add the eggs and mix well, then mix in the Worcestershire sauce, soy sauce, salt, and pepper.
5. Add ½ cup of bread crumbs and mix well. Add more bread crumbs as needed. You only want to add enough bread crumbs to make the mixture stick together; if you add too much, your meatloaf will be dry.
6. Mix in the green peppers and onions.
7. Evenly divide the meatloaf mixture among the 3 mini loaf pans. Gently pat the meat into the pan, so each pan is evenly filled. (Do not pack the pans, just make sure that the meat is evenly distributed in the pan.)
8. Divide the ketchup among the loaf pans and spread it in an even layer over each loaf.
9. Set the temperature to 330°F. Set the timer and bake for 15 minutes.

10. Check if the internal temperature of each meatloaf has reached 160°F. Add more time if needed.

11. Using silicone oven mitts, remove the mini pans from the air fryer and let rest for about 5 minutes before serving.

VARIATION TIP: German meatloaf usually has a couple of hard-boiled eggs diced and stirred into the meatloaf mixture. Another great twist is to substitute ground turkey and chicken for the ground pork and ground beef.

Per Serving: Calories: 618; Fat: 34g; Saturated fat: 14g; Carbohydrate: 28g; Fiber: 2g; Sugar: 8g; Protein: 50g; Iron: 5mg; Sodium: 929mg

AIR FRIED HOMEMADE ITALIAN MEATBALLS

There is nothing like a quick Italian meatball. I always make a batch on Sunday when we have homemade pasta with meatballs, followed by meatball subs on Monday night. Leftovers also make for a quick, filling lunch—topped with marinara or served plain—for any adult or child.

FRY / 400°F

PREP TIME: 10 MINUTES

COOK TIME: 10 MINUTES

SERVES 4 TO 6

---

2 tablespoons olive oil, divided

1 onion, diced

1 pound ground beef

1 pound ground pork

⅓ cup plain bread crumbs

2 large eggs

¼ cup minced fresh parsley

2 teaspoons minced garlic

2 teaspoons salt

1 teaspoon freshly ground black pepper

½ teaspoon red pepper flakes

1 teaspoon Italian seasoning

2 tablespoons grated Parmesan cheese

1. Spray the air fryer basket with olive oil.
2. In a small skillet, heat 1 tablespoon of olive oil over medium-low heat. Add the onions and sauté until soft. Let cool slightly.
3. In a large bowl, mix together the cooked onions, ground beef, ground pork, bread crumbs, eggs, parsley, garlic, salt, black pepper, red pepper flakes, Italian seasoning, and grated Parmesan cheese.
4. Form the mixture into meatballs about 1½ inches in diameter.
5. Place the meatballs in the greased air fryer basket in a single layer. (You may have to cook the meatballs in more than one batch.)
6. Set the temperature to 400°F. Set the timer and fry for 5 minutes.
7. Using tongs, flip the meatballs.
8. Reset the timer and fry for 5 minutes more.

VARIATION TIP: To make a Swedish meatball sauce, combine 1 cup of beef broth, 1 cup of heavy cream, 3 tablespoons of flour, 1 tablespoon of soy sauce, 1 teaspoon of black pepper, and 1 teaspoon of dried rosemary in a small saucepan. Heat the sauce over medium-low heat and simmer for about 10 minutes, stirring constantly. Mix with the meatballs.

Per Serving: Calories: 529; Fat: 35g; Saturated fat: 11g; Carbohydrate: 11g; Fiber: 1g; Sugar: 2g; Protein: 48g; Iron: 4mg; Sodium: 1452mg

EASY AIR FRYER MARINATED PORK TENDERLOIN

FAMILY FAVORITE

This dish can be made up to a day ahead if you need a meal at the ready. The marinade ingredients are common pantry staples that you probably have on hand, so no extra trips to the supermarket are necessary for this dish.

ROASTING / 400°F

PREP TIME: 10 MINUTES, PLUS 1 HOUR TO MARINATE

COOK TIME: 30 MINUTES

SERVES 4 TO 6

¼ cup olive oil

¼ cup soy sauce

¼ cup freshly squeezed lemon juice

1 garlic clove, minced

1 tablespoon Dijon mustard

1 teaspoon salt

½ teaspoon freshly ground black pepper

2 pounds pork tenderloin

1. In a large mixing bowl, make the marinade. Mix together the olive oil, soy sauce, lemon juice, minced garlic, Dijon mustard, salt, and pepper. Reserve ¼ cup of the marinade.
2. Place the tenderloin in a large bowl and pour the remaining marinade over the meat. Cover and marinate in the refrigerator for about 1 hour.
3. Place the marinated pork tenderloin into the air fryer basket.
4. Set the temperature to 400°F. Set the timer and roast for 10 minutes.
5. Using tongs, flip the pork and baste it with half of the reserved marinade.
6. Reset the timer and roast for 10 minutes more.
7. Using tongs, flip the pork, then baste with the remaining marinade.
8. Reset the timer and roast for another 10 minutes, for a total cooking time of 30 minutes.

SUBSTITUTION TIP: Most supermarkets sell premarinated pork tenderloins. If you can find these, buy a couple and keep them in your freezer. For nights when you are pressed for time, use a frozen, premarinated tenderloin. To prepare, skip steps 1 and 2 and add another 10 to 20 minutes to the cooking time.

Per Serving: Calories: 365; Fat: 18g; Saturated fat: 4g; Carbohydrate: 2g; Fiber: 0g; Sugar: 1g; Protein: 49g; Iron: 3mg; Sodium: 1468mg

PERFECT AIR FRIED PORK CHOPS

These breaded pork chops come out of the air fryer fluffy and light, and in only about 20 minutes. Complete this family classic by serving a side of applesauce.

ROAST / 360°F

PREP TIME: 5 MINUTES

COOK TIME: 17 MINUTES

SERVES 4

---

3 cups bread crumbs

½ cup grated Parmesan cheese

2 tablespoons vegetable oil

2 teaspoons salt

2 teaspoons sweet paprika

½ teaspoon onion powder

¼ teaspoon garlic powder

6 (½-inch-thick) bone-in pork chops

1. Spray the air fryer basket with olive oil.

2. In a large resealable bag, combine the bread crumbs, Parmesan cheese, oil, salt, paprika, onion powder, and garlic powder. Seal the bag and shake it a few times in order for the spices to blend together.

3. Place the pork chops, one by one, in the bag and shake to coat.

4. Place the pork chops in the greased air fryer basket in a single layer. Be careful not to overcrowd the basket. (You may have to cook the pork chops in more than one batch.) Spray the chops generously with olive oil to avoid powdery, uncooked breading.

5. Set the temperature to 360°F. Set the timer and roast for 10 minutes.

6. Using tongs, flip the chops. Spray them generously with olive oil.

7. Reset the timer and roast for 7 minutes more.

8. Check that the pork has reached an internal temperature of 145°F. Add cooking time if needed.

SUBSTITUTION TIP: Try making honey garlic pork chops. Instead of coating the chops with breading in steps 2 and 3, simply combine the following in a small mixing bowl: ½ cup of ketchup, 3 tablespoons of honey, 2 tablespoons of soy sauce, 5 teaspoons of minced garlic, and salt and pepper. Brush the sauce over the pork chops and follow the cooking times in the main recipe, but when you flip the pork chops, coat them again with sauce.

Per Serving: Calories: 513; Fat: 23g; Saturated fat: 8g; Carbohydrate: 22g; Fiber: 2g; Sugar: 3g; Protein: 50g; Iron: 3mg; Sodium: 1521mg

AIR FRYER BABY BACK RIBS

FAMILY FAVORITE

From the South, where there is a rib shack on every corner, to the Northeast, where we have chains of rib joints, everyone loves ribs. These ribs go perfectly with homemade mac and cheese and some Air Fried Honey Cornbread (page 106).

GRILL / 400°F

PREP TIME: 5 MINUTES

COOK TIME: 23 TO 25 MINUTES

SERVES 4

___

1 rack baby back ribs

1 tablespoon garlic powder

1 teaspoon freshly ground black pepper

2 tablespoons salt

1 cup barbecue sauce (any type)

1. Dry the ribs with a paper towel.
2. Season the ribs with the garlic powder, pepper, and salt.
3. Place the seasoned ribs into the air fryer.
4. Set the temperature to 400°F. Set the timer and grill for 10 minutes.
5. Using tongs, flip the ribs.
6. Reset the timer and grill for another 10 minutes.
7. Once the ribs are cooked, use a pastry brush to brush on the barbecue sauce, then set the timer and grill for a final 3 to 5 minutes.

___

AIR FRYER TIP: One of the most important tips when making ribs is that you can cut them to fit any air fryer. Just measure out the ribs, then make a cut based on the number of ribs that will fit into it.

___

Per Serving: Calories: 422; Fat: 27g; Saturated fat: 10g; Carbohydrate: 25g; Fiber: 1g; Sugar: 17g; Protein: 18g; Iron: 1mg; Sodium: 4273mg

AIR FRYER LAMB CHOPS

FAMILY FAVORITE, GLUTEN-FREE

You will find most of the ingredients for this recipe in your spice cabinet. Just purchase a couple pounds of lamb chops, and you should be good to go. Lamb chops cook fast and they are filled with flavor; the meat comes from the shoulder, loin, or rib of the animal.

ROAST / 390°F

PREP TIME: 5 MINUTES, PLUS
1 HOUR TO MARINATE

COOK TIME: 7 MINUTES

SERVES 4 TO 6

2 teaspoons dried rosemary

2 teaspoons dried thyme

2 teaspoons dried oregano

2 teaspoons salt

2 teaspoons ground coriander

¼ cup olive oil

¼ cup freshly squeezed lemon juice

2 pounds lamb chops

1. In a large resealable plastic bag, combine the rosemary, thyme, oregano, salt, coriander, olive oil, and lemon juice. Seal the bag and shake to combine.

2. Place the lamb chops into the bag, seal it, and refrigerate for at least 1 hour.

3. Place the lamb chops into the air fryer.

4. Set the temperature to 390°F. Set the timer and roast for 3 minutes.

5. Using tongs, flip the lamb chops.

6. Reset the timer and roast for 4 minutes more for medium-rare. Add 1 to 2 minutes for well-done.

VARIATION TIP: Try serving these with a rosemary sauce. In a small bowl, combine ½ cup of olive oil, 2 tablespoons of soy sauce, 2 tablespoons of balsamic vinegar, 2 tablespoons of dried rosemary, 2 tablespoons of Dijon mustard, and 1 tablespoon of Worcestershire sauce. Next, heat 1 tablespoon of olive oil in a small saucepan over medium heat. Add ¼ cup of diced shallots and 2 teaspoons of minced garlic and sauté until softened. Remove from the heat and mix the garlic and shallot with the rest of the ingredients until well blended. Serve the chops with the sauce for dipping.

Per Serving: Calories: 509; Fat: 34g; Saturated fat: 9g; Carbohydrate: 2g; Fiber: 1g; Sugar: 0g; Protein: 46g; Iron: 5mg; Sodium: 1327mg

AIR FRYER CLASSIC HERB RACK OF LAMB WITH GREEK SEASONINGS

FAMILY FAVORITE, FAST, GLUTEN-FREE

This is one of the most surprising meals I have made for my family in the air fryer. The look of it was so appealing, I appeared to be a gourmet chef in their eyes. The air fryer cooks the meat to the point of perfect tenderness, and the seasonings provide zest to the dish. The exact cooking time of your rack of lamb will depend on how big it is.

ROAST / 360°F

PREP TIME: 5 MINUTES

COOK TIME: 10 MINUTES

SERVES 4

———

¼ cup freshly squeezed lemon juice

1 teaspoon oregano

2 teaspoons minced fresh rosemary

1 teaspoon minced fresh thyme

2 tablespoons minced garlic

Salt

Freshly ground black pepper

2 to 4 tablespoons olive oil

1 lamb rib rack (7 to 8 ribs)

1. In a small mixing bowl, combine the lemon juice, oregano, rosemary, thyme, garlic, salt, pepper, and olive oil and mix well.
2. Rub the mixture over the lamb, covering all of the meat.
3. Place the rack of lamb in the air fryer. (Depending on how big your air fryer is, you may have to remove a rib to make it fit.)
4. Set the temperature to 360°F. Set the timer and roast for 10 minutes.
5. After 10 minutes, measure the internal temperature of the rack of lamb. Medium-rare is 135°F, medium is 145°F, and well-done is 170°F.

AIR FRYER TIP: Rack of lamb is very easy to overcook in the air fryer. My best suggestion would be to check it frequently at even intervals.

Per Serving: Calories: 383; Fat: 26g; Saturated fat: 7g; Carbohydrate: 3g; Fiber: 1g; Sugar: 0g; Protein: 34g; Iron: 3mg; Sodium: 143mg

VEGETABLES AND SIDES

< Air Fried Hasselback Potatoes,
page 104

SIMPLE ROASTED GARLIC ASPARAGUS

FAMILY FAVORITE, FAST, GLUTEN-FREE, VEGAN

This roasted asparagus, tossed with olive oil, salt, and a hint of garlic, is classic and a great side dish for any occasion. It is also a healthy alternative to French fries; you will get a delicious crunch with every bite.

ROAST / 400°F

PREP TIME: 5 MINUTES

COOK TIME: 10 MINUTES

SERVES 4

---

1 pound asparagus

2 tablespoons olive oil

1 tablespoon balsamic vinegar

2 teaspoons minced garlic

Salt

Freshly ground black pepper

1. Cut or snap off the white end of the asparagus.
2. In a large bowl, combine the asparagus, olive oil, vinegar, garlic, salt, and pepper.
3. Using your hands, gently mix all the ingredients together, making sure that the asparagus is thoroughly coated.
4. Lay out the asparagus in the air fryer basket or on an air fryer–size baking sheet set in the basket.
5. Set the temperature to 400°F. Set the timer and roast for 5 minutes.
6. Using tongs, flip the asparagus.
7. Reset the timer and roast for 5 minutes more. (Note, I like my asparagus really soft, so if you like it crispy, roast for less time.)

INGREDIENT TIP: Asparagus is made up of two parts, the green part and the white part. The simplest way to break the stalks apart is to bend the asparagus, which will separate the fresh (edible) part from the stem (known also as the woody end).

Per Serving: Calories: 86; Fat: 7g; Saturated fat: 1g; Carbohydrate: 5g; Fiber: 2g; Sugar: 2g; Protein: 3g; Iron: 2mg; Sodium: 41mg

BROCCOLI WITH PARMESAN CHEESE

FAMILY FAVORITE, FAST, GLUTEN-FREE, VEGETARIAN

How many parents can say that their kids love broccoli? I can. And I give credit to the air fryer and this absolutely delicious roasted broccoli topped with Parmesan cheese. It can be further enhanced by a squeeze of fresh lemon juice just before serving.

STEAM / 360°F

PREP TIME: 5 MINUTES

COOK TIME: 4 MINUTES

SERVES 4

1 pound broccoli florets

2 teaspoons minced garlic

2 tablespoons olive oil

¼ cup grated or shaved Parmesan cheese

1. Preheat the air fryer to 360°F.

2. In a small mixing bowl, mix together the broccoli florets, garlic, olive oil, and Parmesan cheese.

3. Place the broccoli in the air fryer basket in a single layer.

4. Set the timer and steam for 4 minutes.

VARIATION TIP: Try this dish with half cauliflower and half broccoli. Another idea is to add ½ cup of shredded Cheddar cheese to the end of the air frying time. Air fry for about 3 minutes, add the cheese on top, then air fry again just until all the cheese has melted, 1 minute or less.

Per Serving: Calories: 124; Fat: 9g; Saturated fat: 2g; Carbohydrate: 8g; Fiber: 3g; Sugar: 2g; Protein: 6g; Iron: 1mg; Sodium: 103mg

AIR FRIED ROASTED CORN ON THE COB

FAMILY FAVORITE, FAST, GLUTEN-FREE, VEGETARIAN

This is a great air fryer-cooking hack; in fact, it's one of the greatest I have found. There is nothing like fresh corn on the cob with a pat of butter and some salt sprinkled on top. The air fryer gives the corn a great grill-roasted taste, without even turning on the grill. If you cannot fit the corn on the cob in the air fryer basket, simply snap it into two pieces.

GRILL / 400°F

PREP TIME: 5 MINUTES

COOK TIME: 10 MINUTES

SERVES 4

___

1 tablespoon vegetable oil

4 ears of corn, husks and silk removed

Unsalted butter, for topping

Salt, for topping

Freshly ground black pepper, for topping

1. Rub the vegetable oil onto the corn, coating it thoroughly.
2. Set the temperature to 400°F. Set the timer and grill for 5 minutes.
3. Using tongs, flip or rotate the corn.
4. Reset the timer and grill for 5 minutes more.
5. Serve with a pat of butter and a generous sprinkle of salt and pepper.

___

INGREDIENT TIP: You don't have to wait for the summer to enjoy corn on the cob. If you'd like to cook frozen corn on the cob, simply increase the cooking time to 12 minutes, 6 minutes per side.

___

Per Serving: Calories: 265; Fat: 17g; Saturated fat: 8g; Carbohydrate: 29g; Fiber: 4g; Sugar: 5g; Protein: 5g; Iron: 4mg; Sodium: 252mg

AIR FRIED HONEY ROASTED CARROTS

FAMILY FAVORITE, GLUTEN-FREE, VEGETARIAN

This is an easy way to get a healthy side dish on the table in a matter of minutes. I serve these carrots with a sprinkle of fresh dill, which makes the flavor really pop.

ROAST / 390°F

PREP TIME: 5 MINUTES

COOK TIME: 12 MINUTES

SERVES 4

———

3 cups baby carrots

1 tablespoon extra-virgin olive oil

1 tablespoon honey

Salt

Freshly ground black pepper

Fresh dill (optional)

1. In a large bowl, combine the carrots, olive oil, honey, salt, and pepper. Make sure that the carrots are thoroughly coated with oil.
2. Place the carrots in the air fryer basket.
3. Set the temperature to 390°F. Set the timer and roast for 12 minutes, or until fork-tender.
4. Remove the air fryer drawer and release the air fryer basket. Pour the carrots into a bowl, sprinkle with dill, if desired, and serve.

INGREDIENT TIP: For a really easy and fast prep, I purchase the carrots that are already prewashed and precut in the produce section. They usually come in a plastic bag. You can easily omit the honey from this recipe, if you prefer, and still enjoy a delicious basic roasted carrot recipe.

Per Serving: Calories: 80; Fat: 4g; Saturated fat: 1g; Carbohydrate: 13g; Fiber: 2g; Sugar: 8g; Protein: 1g; Iron: 0mg; Sodium: 96mg

AIR FRIED ROASTED CABBAGE

FAMILY FAVORITE, FAST, GLUTEN-FREE, VEGAN

Roasting cabbage brings out its natural sweetness. This side dish pairs wonderfully with any beef or sausage; I usually serve it alongside chicken or Italian sausages. Of course, it is perfect for St. Patrick's Day, with corned beef.

ROAST / 350°F

PREP TIME: 5 MINUTES

COOK TIME: 7 MINUTES

SERVES 4

---

1 head cabbage, sliced in 1-inch-thick ribbons

1 tablespoon olive oil

1 teaspoon salt

1 teaspoon freshly ground black pepper

1 teaspoon garlic powder

1 teaspoon red pepper flakes

1. In a large bowl, combine the cabbage, olive oil, salt, pepper, garlic powder, and red pepper flakes. Make sure that the cabbage is thoroughly coated with oil.

2. Place the cabbage in the air fryer basket.

3. Set the temperature to 350°F. Set the timer and roast for 4 minutes.

4. Using tongs, flip the cabbage.

5. Reset the timer and roast for 3 minutes more.

6. Serve with additional salt, pepper, and/or red pepper flakes, if desired.

AIR FRYER TIP: When making this dish, it is really important that you do not shave your cabbage, as it will end up flying around in the air fryer, causing a potential hazard. You definitely do not want little pieces of cabbage (or other foods) to get lodged in your heating unit. So, keep the cabbage in larger ribbons.

Per Serving: Calories: 78; Fat: 4g; Saturated fat: 1g; Carbohydrate: 11g; Fiber: 5g; Sugar: 6g; Protein: 3g; Iron: 1mg; Sodium: 614mg

AIR FRIED BUFFALO CAULIFLOWER

FAMILY FAVORITE, VEGETARIAN

Roasting cauliflower in the air fryer gives it a perfect combination of textures—both crispy and tender. This is a versatile recipe, and you can change the cauliflower out for broccoli, or better yet, do a mixture of half cauliflower and half broccoli.

ROAST / 350°F

PREP TIME: 5 MINUTES

COOK TIME: 13 MINUTES

SERVES 4

---

4 tablespoons (½ stick) unsalted butter, melted

¼ cup buffalo wing sauce

4 cups cauliflower florets

1 cup panko bread crumbs

1. Spray the air fryer basket with olive oil.
2. In a small bowl, mix the melted butter with the buffalo wing sauce.
3. Put the panko bread crumbs in a separate small bowl.
4. Dip the cauliflower in the sauce, making sure to coat the top of the cauliflower, then dip the cauliflower in the panko.
5. Place the cauliflower into the greased air fryer basket, being careful not to overcrowd them. Spray the cauliflower generously with olive oil.
6. Set the temperature to 350°F. Set the timer and roast for 7 minutes.
7. Using tongs, flip the cauliflower. Spray generously with olive oil.
8. Reset the timer and roast for another 6 minutes.

AIR FRYER TIP: When cooking any food with breading, it is really important that the coating gets sprayed generously with olive oil, because otherwise the breading will become dry and powdery. I can't emphasize this enough: Always spray generously, until the item appears wet all over, so you get a nicely cooked, crispy, and tasty final product.

Per Serving: Calories: 234; Fat: 13g; Saturated fat: 8g; Carbohydrate: 25g; Fiber: 4g; Sugar: 4g; Protein: 4g; Iron: 2mg; Sodium: 333mg

SWEET POTATO FRENCH FRIES

FAMILY FAVORITE, GLUTEN-FREE, VEGAN

I love sweet potato fries. I used to only order sweet potato fries when I went out to restaurants because I didn't know how to make them at home. Now, armed with my air fryer, I have become a French fry pro. These can be jazzed up by any seasoning; my family loves them with Cajun spice. I prefer them plain with a heap of ketchup. You will be amazed at how easy they are to make.

FRY / 380°F

PREP TIME: 5 MINUTES

COOK TIME: 20 TO 22 MINUTES

SERVES 4

---

2 sweet potatoes

1 teaspoon salt

½ teaspoon freshly ground black pepper

2 teaspoons olive oil

1. Preheat the air fryer to 380°F.
2. Cut the sweet potatoes lengthwise into ½-inch-thick slices. Then cut each slice into ½-inch-thick fries.
3. In a small mixing bowl, toss the sweet potato fries with the salt, pepper, and olive oil, making sure that all the potatoes are thoroughly coated with oil. Add more oil as needed.
4. Place the potatoes in the air fryer basket.
5. Set the timer and fry for 20 minutes. Shake the basket several times during cooking so that the fries will be evenly cooked and crisp.
6. Open the air fryer drawer and release the basket. Pour the potatoes into a serving bowl and toss with additional salt and pepper, if desired.

SUBSTITUTION TIP: To make homemade French fries using ordinary potatoes, use 2 russet potatoes instead of the sweet potatoes. Follow the recipe as instructed but cook for only 12 to 15 minutes. And don't forget to shake the basket a few times during cooking.

Per Serving: Calories: 77; Fat: 2g; Saturated fat: 0g; Carbohydrate: 13g; Fiber: 2g; Sugar: 3g; Protein: 1g; Iron: 0mg; Sodium: 612mg

AIR FRIED ROASTED SWEET POTATOES

FAMILY FAVORITE, GLUTEN-FREE, VEGAN

These roasted sweet potatoes come out a bit crispy on the outside but soft in the middle. I serve my sweet potatoes with a pat of butter and a tablespoon or two of brown sugar. For added flavor, you can make this spice mix and rub it on the outside of the potatoes before cooking: 1 teaspoon of salt, ¼ teaspoon of freshly ground black pepper, ½ teaspoon of chili powder, ½ teaspoon of paprika, ½ teaspoon of ground cumin, and ½ teaspoon of garlic powder.

ROAST / 400°F

PREP TIME: 10 MINUTES

COOK TIME: 30 TO 45 MINUTES

SERVES 4

———

4 sweet potatoes

¼ cup olive oil

2 teaspoons salt

½ teaspoon freshly ground black pepper

1. Use a fork to poke a few holes in each of the sweet potatoes.
2. Rub the skins of the sweet potatoes with olive oil, salt, and pepper.
3. Place the coated sweet potatoes in the air fryer basket.
4. Set the temperature to 400°F. Set the timer and roast for 15 minutes.
5. Using tongs, flip or rotate the potatoes.
6. Reset the timer and roast for another 15 minutes. Check to see if the sweet potatoes are fork-tender. If not, add up to 15 minutes more. (The cooking time will depend on how large the sweet potatoes are.)

SUBSTITUTION TIP: To make roasted potatoes, substitute 4 russet potatoes for the sweet potatoes. Follow the same instructions as above but increase the total cooking time to 50 minutes. I like to roll my roasted potatoes in olive oil and sea salt. I love the flavor of those two in the air fryer.

Per Serving: Calories: 220; Fat: 13g; Saturated fat: 2g; Carbohydrate: 26g; Fiber: 4g; Sugar: 5g; Protein: 2g; Iron: 1mg; Sodium: 1234mg

AIR FRIED HASSELBACK POTATOES

FAMILY FAVORITE, GLUTEN-FREE, VEGETARIAN

What a fun way to serve potatoes to kids! They love that they are "fancy" potatoes, but they are still completely approachable. They cook faster than regular potatoes, since they are sliced open, and they are a bit crispy. Experiment with layering different ingredients between the slices, such as herb butter or cheese.

BAKE / 350°F

PREP TIME: 10 MINUTES

COOK TIME: 35 MINUTES

SERVES 4

---

4 russet potatoes

2 tablespoons olive oil

1 teaspoon salt

½ teaspoon freshly ground black pepper

¼ cup grated Parmesan cheese

1. Without cutting all the way through the bottom of the potato (so the slices stay connected), cut each potato into ½-inch-wide horizontal slices.

2. Brush the potatoes thoroughly with olive oil, being careful to brush in between all the slices. Season with salt and pepper.

3. Place the potatoes in the air fryer basket.

4. Set the temperature to 350°F. Set the timer and bake for 20 minutes.

5. Brush more olive oil onto the potatoes.

6. Reset the timer and bake for 15 minutes more. Remove the potatoes when they are fork-tender.

7. Sprinkle the cooked potatoes with salt, pepper, and Parmesan cheese.

SUBSTITUTION TIP: Using the same Hasselback method, switch out the russet potatoes for sweet potatoes. In a small mixing bowl, mix together 1 tablespoon of melted butter, 1 teaspoon of olive oil, and 1 teaspoon of minced fresh thyme and rub the mixture all over the sweet potatoes. Serve with additional butter and salt.

Per Serving: Calories: 230; Fat: 9g; Saturated fat: 2g; Carbohydrate: 34g; Fiber: 5g; Sugar: 3g; Protein: 6g; Iron: 1mg; Sodium: 659mg

ROASTED ROSEMARY POTATOES

FAMILY FAVORITE, GLUTEN-FREE, VEGAN

The air fryer does a great job roasting potatoes. This classic dish can be served alongside any protein but is especially good with roast chicken or beef. The rosemary and garlic are versatile flavors that help make these roasted potatoes a go-to side dish for almost any meal.

ROAST / 400°F

PREP TIME: 5 MINUTES

COOK TIME: 20 TO 22 MINUTES

SERVES 4

1½ pounds small red potatoes, cut into 1-inch cubes

2 tablespoons olive oil

1 teaspoon salt

½ teaspoon freshly ground black pepper

1 tablespoon minced garlic

2 tablespoons minced fresh rosemary

1. Preheat the air fryer to 400°F.
2. In a medium mixing bowl, combine the diced potatoes, olive oil, salt, pepper, minced garlic, and rosemary and mix well, so the potatoes are thoroughly coated with olive oil.
3. Place the potatoes into the air fryer basket in a single layer.
4. Set the timer and roast for 20 to 22 minutes. Every 5 minutes, remove the air fryer drawer and shake, so the potatoes redistribute in the basket for even cooking.
5. Remove the air fryer drawer and release the basket. Pour the potatoes into a large serving bowl, toss with additional salt and pepper, and serve.

SUBSTITUTION TIP: Switch out the red potatoes for about 2 pounds of sweet potatoes, cut into 1-inch cubes. Toss the sweet potatoes with 2 tablespoons of olive oil, 1 teaspoon of salt, and 1 tablespoon of brown sugar. Proceed with steps 3 through 5, but increase the cooking time to 25 minutes.

Per Serving: Calories: 182; Fat: 7g; Saturated fat: 1g; Carbohydrate: 29g; Fiber: 4g; Sugar: 2g; Protein: 4g; Iron: 2mg; Sodium: 593mg

AIR FRIED HONEY CORNBREAD

FAMILY FAVORITE, VEGETARIAN

The sweet honey flavor of this cornbread is what keeps the kids coming back for more. And I am more than happy to make it, because it couldn't be easier in the air fryer. Serve it with melted butter and a drizzle of honey.

BAKE / 360°F

PREP TIME: 5 MINUTES

COOK TIME: 20 TO 24 MINUTES

SERVES 4

---

1 cup all-purpose flour

1 cup yellow cornmeal

½ cup sugar

1 teaspoon salt

2 teaspoons baking powder

1 large egg

1 cup milk

⅓ cup vegetable oil

¼ cup honey

1. Spray an air fryer–safe baking pan (square or round) with olive oil or cooking spray.
2. In a large mixing bowl, combine the flour, cornmeal, sugar, salt, baking powder, egg, milk, oil, and honey and mix lightly.
3. Pour the cornbread batter into the prepared pan.
4. Set the temperature to 360°F. Set the timer and bake for 20 minutes.
5. Insert a toothpick into the center of the cornbread to make sure the middle is cooked; if not, bake for another 3 to 4 minutes.
6. Using silicone oven mitts, remove the pan from the air fryer and let cool slightly. Serve warm.

COOKING TIP: If the top of the bread is completely cooked, but the bottom or center is not done, simply flip the cornbread over and set the timer for another 4 to 5 minutes.

Per Serving: Calories: 594; Fat: 22g; Saturated fat: 5g; Carbohydrate: 94g; Fiber: 3g; Sugar: 46g; Protein: 9g; Iron: 3mg; Sodium: 642mg

DESSERTS

< Easy Air Fried Old-Fashioned Cherry Cobbler,
page 117

AIR FRYER HOMEMADE PUMPKIN FRITTERS

FAMILY FAVORITE, FAST, VEGETARIAN

Pumpkin fritters are an awesome fall dessert. They also make a wonderful breakfast. Serve them with a dash of cinnamon-sugar and a side of cream cheese, and you'll have the perfect treat to go with your morning or evening coffee.

BAKE / 330°F

PREP TIME: 5 MINUTES

COOK TIME: 7 TO 9 MINUTES

MAKES 8 FRITTERS

FOR THE FRITTERS

1 (16.3-ounce, 8-count) package refrigerated biscuit dough

½ cup chopped pecans

¼ cup pumpkin purée

¼ cup sugar

1 teaspoon pumpkin pie spice

2 tablespoons unsalted butter, melted

FOR THE GLAZE

1 cup powdered sugar

1 teaspoon pumpkin pie spice

1 tablespoon pumpkin purée

2 tablespoons milk (plus more to thin the glaze, if necessary)

TO MAKE THE FRITTERS

1. Spray the air fryer basket with olive oil or spray an air fryer–size baking sheet with olive oil or cooking spray.

2. Turn the biscuit dough out onto a cutting board.

3. Cut each biscuit into 8 pieces.

4. Once you cut all the pieces, place them in a medium mixing bowl.

5. Add the pecans, pumpkin, sugar, and pumpkin pie spice to the biscuit pieces and toss until well combined.

6. Shape the dough into 8 even mounds.

7. Drizzle butter over each of the fritters. (This will help them stay together as you air fry them.)

8. Place the fritters directly in the greased air fryer basket, or on the greased baking sheet set in the air fryer basket.

9. Set the temperature to 330°F. Set the timer and bake for 7 minutes.

10. Check to see if the fritters are done. The dough should be cooked through and solid to the touch. If not, cook for 1 to 2 minutes more.

11. Using tongs, gently remove the fritters from the air fryer. Let cool for about 10 minutes before you apply the glaze.

TO MAKE THE GLAZE

1. In a small mixing bowl, mix together the powdered sugar, pumpkin pie spice, pumpkin, and milk until smooth. If it seems more like icing, it is too thick. It should coat a spoon and be of a pourable consistency.

2. Drizzle the glaze over the fritters.

VARIATION TIP: To make apple fritters, in a small mixing bowl, mix together ½ cup of sugar and 1 teaspoon of ground cinnamon. In another small mixing bowl, combine 1 cup of peeled and diced apple, 4 tablespoons of melted butter, and 2 tablespoons of the cinnamon-sugar. Roll out the dough from 1 package of refrigerated biscuit dough. Place a heaping tablespoon of the apple mixture in the middle of each biscuit. Roll the dough back up, then dip each fritter into the remaining cinnamon-sugar. Follow steps 7 through 11 in the main recipe.

Per Serving (1 fritter): Calories: 341; Fat: 16g; Saturated fat: 5g; Carbohydrate: 47g; Fiber: 2g; Sugar: 26g; Protein: 5g; Iron: 2mg; Sodium: 608mg

EASY CHOCOLATE-FROSTED DOUGHNUTS

FAMILY FAVORITE, FAST, VEGETARIAN

This was one of my first air fryer experiments. One word: easy! This is a typical Southern breakfast, usually deep-fried in a vat of oil, but now you can make a healthier version with your air fryer. The chocolate glaze adds the finishing touch. Feel free to add sprinkles.

BAKE / 330°F

PREP TIME: 5 MINUTES

COOK TIME: 5 MINUTES

MAKES 8 DOUGHNUTS

---

1 (16.3-ounce / 8-count) package refrigerated biscuit dough

¾ cup powdered sugar

¼ cup unsweetened cocoa powder

¼ cup milk

1. Spray the air fryer basket with olive oil.
2. Unroll the biscuit dough onto a cutting board and separate the biscuits.
3. Using a 1-inch biscuit cutter or cookie cutter, cut out the center of each biscuit.
4. Place the doughnuts into the air fryer. (You may have to cook your doughnuts in more than one batch.)
5. Set the temperature to 330°F. Set the timer and bake for 5 minutes.
6. Using tongs, remove the doughnuts from the air fryer and let them cool slightly before glazing.
7. Meanwhile, in a small mixing bowl, combine the powdered sugar, unsweetened cocoa powder, and milk and mix until smooth.
8. Dip your doughnuts into the glaze and use a knife to smooth the frosting evenly over the doughnut.
9. Let the glaze set before serving.

SUBSTITUTION TIP: If you prefer vanilla glaze, in step 7, mix together 1 cup of powdered sugar, ¼ cup of milk, and ½ teaspoon of vanilla extract, then proceed with the recipe as instructed.

Per Serving (1 doughnut): Calories: 233; Fat: 8g; Saturated fat: 3g; Carbohydrate: 37g; Fiber: 2g; Sugar: 15g; Protein: 5g; Iron: 2mg; Sodium: 590mg

AIR FRYER HOMEMADE CHOCOLATE CHIP COOKIES

FAMILY FAVORITE, FAST, VEGETARIAN

Who doesn't love homemade chocolate chip cookies? We all have fond memories of this classic cookie. You can make the dough ahead of time and keep it refrigerated for a few days and always have homemade chocolate chip cookies on hand.

BAKE / 340°F

PREP TIME: 5 MINUTES

COOK TIME: 5 MINUTES

MAKES 25 COOKIES

1 cup (2 sticks) unsalted butter, at room temperature

1 cup granulated sugar

1 cup brown sugar

2 large eggs

½ teaspoon vanilla extract

1 teaspoon baking soda

½ teaspoon salt

3 cups all-purpose flour

2 cups chocolate chips

1. Spray an air fryer–size baking sheet with cooking spray. (If you want to cook the cookies directly in the basket, see the tip below.)
2. In a large bowl, cream the butter and both sugars.
3. Mix in the eggs, vanilla, baking soda, salt, and flour until well combined. Fold in the chocolate chips.
4. Use your hands and knead the dough together, so everything is well mixed.
5. Using a cookie scoop or a tablespoon, drop heaping spoonfuls of dough onto the baking sheet about 1 inch apart. (You may need to bake the cookies in more than one batch.)
6. Set the baking sheet into the air fryer.
7. Set the temperature to 340°F. Set the timer and bake for 5 minutes.
8. When the cookies are golden brown and cooked through, use silicone oven mitts to remove the baking sheet from the air fryer and serve.

COOKING TIP: If you line your air fryer basket with air fryer parchment paper sprayed with cooking spray, you can cook multiple batches of cookies with very little cleanup.

Per Serving (1 cookie): Calories: 280; Fat: 13g; Saturated fat: 8g; Carbohydrate: 38g; Fiber: 0g; Sugar: 24g; Protein: 3g; Iron: 1mg; Sodium: 156mg

AIR FRYER STUFFED BAKED APPLES

FAMILY FAVORITE, GLUTEN-FREE, VEGETARIAN

I always make this dessert after our yearly apple-picking day in September. You can use any type of apple. I love the richness of the apple, and I always add a bit of maple syrup over mine. My kids prefer it with a scoop of vanilla ice cream on the side. However you eat these, they will soon be one of your favorite desserts.

BAKE / 350°F

PREP TIME: 5 MINUTES

COOK TIME: 20 MINUTES

SERVES 4

———

4 to 6 tablespoons chopped walnuts

4 to 6 tablespoons raisins

4 tablespoons (½ stick) unsalted butter, melted

1 teaspoon ground cinnamon

½ teaspoon ground nutmeg

4 apples, cored but with the bottoms left intact

Vanilla ice cream, for topping

Maple syrup, for topping

1. In a small mixing bowl, make the filling. Mix together the walnuts, raisins, melted butter, cinnamon, and nutmeg.
2. Scoop a quarter of the filling into each apple.
3. Place the apples in an air fryer–safe pan and set the pan in the air fryer basket.
4. Set the temperature to 350°F. Set the timer and bake for 20 minutes.
5. Serve with vanilla ice cream and a drizzle of maple syrup.

VARIATION TIP: If you'd like to make baked apples with oatmeal filling, just add 1 cup of rolled oats and ¼ cup of brown sugar to the filling.

Per Serving: Calories: 382; Fat: 19g; Saturated fat: 9g; Carbohydrate: 57g; Fiber: 7g; Sugar: 44g; Protein: 4g; Iron: 2mg; Sodium: 100mg

EASY AIR FRIED APPLE HAND PIES

FAMILY FAVORITE, FAST, VEGETARIAN

This is the perfect dessert, and it makes an amazing lunch box snack. You will love the flaky crust and warm apple filling. These will be eaten quicker than you can make them.

BAKE / 350°F

PREP TIME: 5 MINUTES

COOK TIME: 7 MINUTES

MAKES 8 HAND PIES

---

1 package prepared pie dough

½ cup apple pie filling

1 large egg white

1 tablespoon Wilton White Sparkling Sugar

Caramel sauce, for drizzling

1. Spray the air fryer basket with olive oil.
2. Lightly flour a clean work surface. Lay out the dough on the work surface.
3. Using a 2-inch biscuit cutter, cut out 8 circles from the dough.
4. Gather up the scraps of dough, form them into a ball, and reroll them. Using the biscuit cutter, cut out the remaining dough.
5. Add about 1 tablespoon of apple pie filling to the center of each circle.
6. Fold over the dough and use a fork to seal the edges.
7. Brush the egg white over the top, then sprinkle with sparkling sugar.
8. Place the hand pies in the greased air fryer basket. They should be spaced so that they do not touch one another. (You may need to cook the hand pies in more than one batch.)
9. Set the temperature to 350°F. Set the timer and bake for 5 minutes. When they are done, the crust should be golden brown. If they are not done, bake for another 2 minutes. Drizzle with caramel sauce, if desired.

SUBSTITUTION TIP: Swap out the apple pie filling for cherry or blueberries—or add a tablespoon of Nutella and a couple of mini marshmallows for a s'mores-style hand pie.

Per Serving (1 pie): Calories: 120; Fat: 5g; Saturated fat: 1g; Carbohydrate: 17g; Fiber: 0g; Sugar: 3g; Protein: 1g; Iron: 0mg; Sodium: 144mg

EASY AIR FRYER BLUEBERRY PIE

FAMILY FAVORITE, VEGETARIAN

Another American classic dessert, this pie can even be made on a weekday when you are pressed for time. In the summer, make it after berry-picking; just replace the pie filling with 3 to 4 cups of fresh berries and ½ cup of sugar.

BAKE / 310°F

PREP TIME: 5 MINUTES, PLUS 30 MINUTES TO THAW

COOK TIME: 15 TO 18 MINUTES

SERVES 4 TO 6

---

2 frozen pie crusts

2 (21-ounce) jars blueberry pie filling

1 teaspoon milk

1 teaspoon sugar

1. Remove the pie crusts from the freezer and let them thaw for 30 minutes on the countertop.
2. Place one crust into the bottom of a 6-inch pie pan.
3. Pour the pie filling into the bottom crust, then cover it with the other crust, being careful to press the bottom and top crusts together around the edge to form a seal.
4. Trim off any excess pie dough.
5. Cut venting holes in the top crust with a knife or a small decoratively shaped cookie cutter.
6. Brush the top crust with milk, then sprinkle the sugar over it.
7. Place the pie in the air fryer basket.
8. Set the temperature to 310°F. Set the timer and bake for 15 minutes.
9. Check the pie after 15 minutes. If it needs additional time, reset the timer and bake for an additional 3 minutes.
10. Using silicone oven mitts, remove the pie from the air fryer and let cool for 15 minutes before serving.

VARIATION TIP: To make a homemade pie crust, combine 1 cup (2 sticks) of cold butter, 2½ cups of flour, 1 teaspoon of salt, and ¼ cup of ice water in a stand mixer or food processor. Form the dough into 2 round balls. Lightly flour a clean work surface and roll out each ball of dough until it's between 9 and 10 inches in diameter. Proceed with the recipe from step 2, as instructed.

Per Serving: Calories: 537; Fat: 14g; Saturated fat: 2g; Carbohydrate: 101g; Fiber: 3g; Sugar: 58g; Protein: 2g; Iron: 1mg; Sodium: 313mg

EASY AIR FRIED OLD-FASHIONED CHERRY COBBLER

FAMILY FAVORITE, VEGETARIAN

Cherry cobbler is a delicious treat, whether in the summertime or in the middle of winter. It's a perfect dessert that the whole family will love. I typically serve it on Sunday morning with a hot cup of coffee for the adults and a warm cup of hot chocolate for the kids.

BAKE / 320°F

PREP TIME: 5 MINUTES

COOK TIME: 30 TO 35 MINUTES

SERVES 4

———————

1 cup all-purpose flour

1 cup sugar

2 tablespoons baking powder

¾ cup milk

8 tablespoons (1 stick) unsalted butter

1 (21-ounce) can cherry pie filling

1. In a small mixing bowl, mix together the flour, sugar, and baking powder. Add the milk and mix until well blended.

2. Melt the butter in a small microwave-safe bowl in the microwave, about 45 seconds.

3. Pour the butter into the bottom of an 8-by-8-inch pan, then pour in the batter and spread it in an even layer. Pour the pie filing over the batter. Do not mix; the batter will bubble up through the filling during cooking.

4. Set the temperature to 320°F. Set the timer and bake for 20 minutes.

5. Check the cobbler. When the cobbler is done the batter will be golden brown and cooked through. If not done, bake and recheck for doneness in 5-minute intervals. Overall cooking time will likely be between 30 and 35 minutes.

6. Remove from the air fryer and let cool slightly before serving.

SUBSTITUTION TIP: Be mindful of the kind of pan you use, as you don't want one that makes direct contact with the air fryer's heating element. You can also use a piece of aluminum foil to cover your cobbler to prevent burning.

Per Serving: Calories: 706; Fat: 24g; Saturated fat: 15g; Carbohydrate: 121g; Fiber: 2g; Sugar: 52g; Protein: 6g; Iron: 2mg; Sodium: 219mg

AIR FRYER BANANA CAKE

FAMILY FAVORITE, VEGETARIAN

Banana cake has a lovely texture to it, similar to banana bread but more textured like a cake. I often serve this cake topped with a cream cheese frosting. I love that it's relatively healthy and I always find a great way to use up ripened bananas, which is a great money-saver.

BAKE / 320° F

PREP TIME: 5 MINUTES

COOK TIME: 30 MINUTES

SERVES 4

───────

⅓ cup brown sugar

4 tablespoons (½ stick) unsalted butter, at room temperature

1 ripe banana, mashed

1 large egg

2 tablespoons granulated sugar

1 cup all-purpose flour

1 teaspoon ground cinnamon

1 teaspoon vanilla extract

½ teaspoon ground nutmeg

1. Spray a 6-inch Bundt pan with cooking spray.
2. In a medium mixing bowl, cream the brown sugar and butter until pale and fluffy.
3. Mix in the banana and egg.
4. Add the granulated sugar, flour, ground cinnamon, vanilla, and nutmeg and mix well.
5. Spoon the batter into the prepared pan.
6. Place the pan in the air fryer basket.
7. Set the temperature to 320°F. Set the timer and bake for 15 minutes.
8. Do a toothpick test. If the toothpick comes out clean, the cake is done. It there is batter on the toothpick, cook and check again in 5-minute intervals until the cake is done. It will likely take about 30 minutes total baking time to fully cook.
9. Using silicone oven mitts, remove the Bundt pan from the air fryer.

10. Set the pan on a wire cooling rack and let cool for about 10 minutes. Place a plate upside-down (like a lid) over the top of the Bundt pan. Carefully flip the plate and the pan over, and set the plate on the counter. Lift the Bundt pan off the cake. Frost as desired.

AIR FRYER TIP: Bundt pans are perfect for the air fryer, since you don't have to worry about making sure the middle gets cooked. To use a Bundt pan for your air fryer, simply purchase one that is slightly smaller than the size of your air fryer basket.

Per Serving: Calories: 334; Fat: 13g; Saturated fat: 8g; Carbohydrate: 49g; Fiber: 2g; Sugar: 22g; Protein: 5g; Iron: 2mg; Sodium: 104mg

CHOCOLATE BUNDT CAKE

FAMILY FAVORITE, VEGETARIAN

This is the perfect beginner's recipe for making a homemade cake. But be forewarned, you will be addicted to making cakes because they come out so light and fluffy from the air fryer. Top with a rich chocolate frosting for an amazing and decadent dessert.

BAKE / 330°F

PREP TIME: 5 MINUTES

COOK TIME: 30 MINUTES

SERVES 4

1¾ cups all-purpose flour

2 cups sugar

¾ cup unsweetened cocoa powder

1 teaspoon baking soda

1 teaspoon baking powder

½ cup vegetable oil

1 teaspoon salt

2 teaspoons vanilla extract

2 large eggs

1 cup milk

1 cup hot water

1. Spray a 6-inch Bundt pan with cooking spray.
2. In a large mixing bowl, combine the flour, sugar, cocoa powder, baking soda, baking powder, oil, salt, vanilla, eggs, milk, and hot water.
3. Pour the cake batter into the prepared pan and set the pan in the air fryer basket.
4. Set the temperature to 330°F. Set the timer and bake for 20 minutes.
5. Do a toothpick test. If the toothpick comes out clean, the cake is done. It there is batter on the toothpick, cook and check again in 5-minute intervals until the cake is done. It will likely take about 30 minutes total baking time to fully cook.
6. Using silicone oven mitts, remove the Bundt pan from the air fryer.
7. Set the pan on a wire cooling rack and let cool for about 10 minutes. Place a plate upside down (like a lid) over the top of the Bundt pan. Carefully flip the plate and the pan over, and set the plate on the counter. Lift the Bundt pan off the cake.

VARIATION TIP: For a great chocolate frosting, in a small mixing bowl, combine 8 tablespoons (1 stick) of melted butter, ⅔ cup of unsweetened cocoa powder, 3 cups of powdered sugar, ⅓ cup of milk, and 1 teaspoon of vanilla extract. Mix until smooth.

Per Serving: Calories: 924; Fat: 34g; Saturated fat: 6g; Carbohydrate: 155g; Fiber: 6g; Sugar: 104g; Protein: 14g; Iron: 6mg; Sodium: 965mg

HOMEMADE AIR FRIED FUDGE BROWNIES

FAMILY FAVORITE, VEGETARIAN

These are really awesome fudge brownies. When my kids have friends over, this is what they ask me to make. This dessert will soon become a staple in your family's life and is great for any holiday or potluck dinner.

BAKE / 350°F

PREP TIME: 5 MINUTES

COOK TIME: 20 MINUTES

SERVES 6

8 tablespoons (1 stick) unsalted butter, melted

1 cup sugar

1 teaspoon vanilla extract

2 large eggs

½ cup all-purpose flour

½ cup cocoa powder

1 teaspoon baking powder

1. Spray a 6-inch air fryer–safe baking pan with cooking spray or grease the pan with butter.
2. In a medium mixing bowl, mix together the butter and sugar, then add the vanilla and eggs and beat until well combined.
3. Add the flour, cocoa powder, and baking powder and mix until smooth.
4. Pour the batter into the prepared pan.
5. Set the temperature to 350°F. Set the timer and bake for 20 minutes. Once the center is set, use silicon oven mitts to remove the pan from the air fryer.
6. Let cool slightly before serving.

AIR FRYER TIP: To make brownies from any store-bought mix, simply follow the instructions on the box, then pour the batter into a prepared air fryer–safe pan and set the temperature to 350°F. Cook for about 15 minutes or until the toothpick comes out clean.

Per Serving: Calories: 338; Fat: 18g; Saturated fat: 11g; Carbohydrate: 46g; Fiber: 2g; Sugar: 34g; Protein: 4g; Iron: 2mg; Sodium: 132mg

Resources

Here are some great resources that will help you learn about air fryers; these companies provide a lot of information about how to use their products. But remember it's always best to look up your manufacturer's website for the accurate information for your machine.

GoWise Air Fryer: https://www.gowiseproducts.com
A comprehensive site hosted by the air fryer manufacturer GoWise. On this site, you can shop for air fryers, review owner manuals, watch the GoWise YouTube channel, or find recipes.

Philips Air Fryer: https://www.usa.philips.com/c-m-ho/cooking/airfryer-xxl
This air fryer manufacturer has everything you need from product specifications to owner manuals to a free recipe booklet.

Instant Pot: https://instantappliances.com/
The latest manufacturer to start producing air fryers, Instant Pot offers a free app for recipes, as well as recipes online, easy access to owner's manuals, and troubleshooting support.

Here is a great place to gather recipes specifically for the air fryer:

ForkToSpoon.com: This is my own site, which focuses on air fryer recipes, including cakes, brownies, and other delicious baked goods. I use very easy and accessible products for my recipes.

> Air Fryer Grilled Chicken Fajitas, page 66

Index

Acknowledgments

I would like to thank the faithful readers of my website, ForkToSpoon.com, and the love and support over the past few years from our Facebook group, Air Fryer Tips and Recipes, which originally had 70 struggling air fryer users, but at the publication of this book has over half a million.

About the Author

LAURIE FLEMING is a recipe developer and food blogger at ForkToSpoon.com. She has been featured on MSN, AOL, BuzzFeed, Southern Made Simple, KrazyCoupon-Lady, and other publications. Laurie lives in Philadelphia with her family.

Printed in the USA
CPSIA information can be obtained
at www.ICGtesting.com
LVHW071505041123
762724LV00002B/19

9 781646 111510